## THE BIG BOOK OF
## QUESTIONS & ANSWERS
# SAVE THE EARTH

Linda Schwartz

Consultant: Elissa Wolfson

PUBLICATIONS INTERNATIONAL, LTD.

Illustrated by:
T.F. Marsh
Joe Veno

Writer Linda Schwartz has authored over 60 educational and activity books for children including *Earth Book for Kids: Activities to Help Heal the Environment* and *My Earth Book*. She is a former school teacher and currently president of Educational Consulting Works and The Learning Works, Inc.

Consultant Elissa Wolfson is Managing Editor of *E: The Environmental Magazine* and has an M.A. in Environmental Studies from Montclair State College and a B.S. in Environmental Education from Cornell University. She has been active in environmental research and education for organizations including the New York Zoological Society, Institute of Ecosystem Studies, and the Audubon Expedition Institute.

Special thanks to Phyllis Amerikaner

# CONTENTS

# UNDERSTANDING OUR EARTH

**Q. What is Earth?**

**A.** *Earth* is our planet. Of the nine planets that orbit our sun, Earth is the third closest to the sun and the fifth largest in size. Earth is covered with water, soil, and rock. It is the only planet we know of that supports living things, including plants, animals, and over five billion people. Earth gives us air, food, water, and shelter. Earth is our home.

**Q. What does environment mean?**

**A.** An *environment* is everything, both living and nonliving, that surrounds us and affects us. This includes the sun that shines, the air we breathe, and the weather that changes. It is wind and clouds, wildflowers and cornfields, insects and hippos, delicate sea shells and huge rocks. A person who cares about the environment is an *environmentalist*.

**Q. In what ways do we depend on our environment?**

**A.** We depend on our environment for the things we use to make wheat bread, cotton shirts, and brick houses. We depend on our environment for the water we use for drinking, swimming, fishing, and gardening. We depend on our environment for the beauty of a quiet sunset, a clear river, or an ancient forest. We depend on our environment for life.

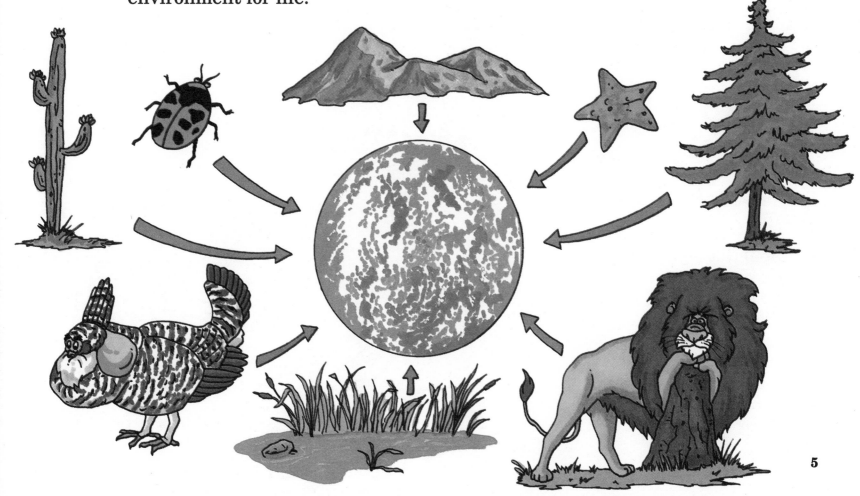

**Q. What is ecology?**

**A.** *Ecology* is the study of the way plants and animals depend on their environment and on each other to exist. For example, trees need sunlight, air, water, and good soil to grow. When a tree drops its leaves to the ground, some of these leaves will be used by animals for nests or for food. If the leaves stay on the ground and rot, they will become new soil for other plants. People who study ecology are *ecologists*.

**Q. Why is the study of ecology important?**

**A.** Ecologists try to learn more about the way our Earth supports life. By studying how living things affect one another and the environment around them, they can find ways to solve many of the problems facing our planet today. Many ecologists study the way people affect the Earth and the other creatures that live here with us.

**Q. What is an ecosystem?**

**A.** An *ecosystem* consists of all the living and nonliving things in a particular area. Ecosystems include plants and animals, as well as air, water, soil, climate, and energy. Prairies, forests, fields, and lakes are all examples of ecosystems.

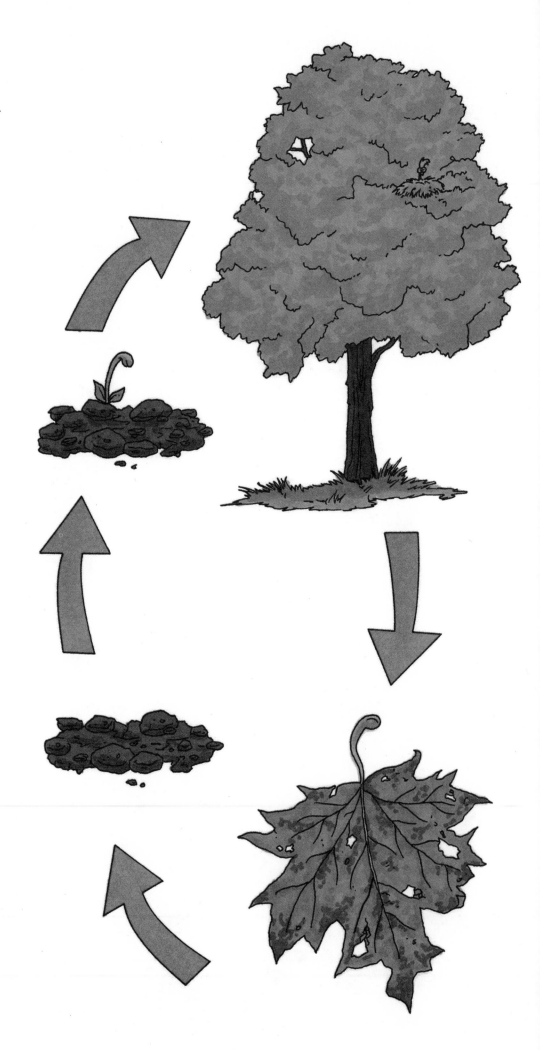

6

**RENEWABLE RESOURCES**

**NONRENEWABLE RESOURCES**

OIL

**Q. What are natural resources?**

**A.** *Natural resources* are things on our Earth that help support life. Land, water, and air are natural resources that we need to live. Some people think of the plants and animals we use for food, clothing, shelter, and medicines as natural resources. Natural resources also include oil, coal, and even sunshine, which we use for fuel to run our cars and heat our homes in the winter.

**Q. What are renewable resources?**

**A.** *Renewable resources* are things that we can use and then replace. When we harvest a crop of pumpkins, the seeds inside the pumpkins can grow into new pumpkin plants. When we clip a sheep to make wool, the sheep grows a new coat that we can clip again next year. Nature has ways to replace resources such as these, so they are renewable.

**Q. What are nonrenewable resources?**

**A.** *Nonrenewable resources* cannot be replaced. The sun is an example of a resource that cannot be replaced. Coal and oil are made from fossils, which take millions of years to form. They are also nonrenewable resources. Today, we are using many of our resources faster than nature can create them.

**Q. How did the invention of machines affect our environment?**

**A.** With the invention of machines, humans began to use more of the Earth's resources to build the machines and to run them. With machines, it was easier to clear the land, use river water, and hunt animals. Factories dumped waste into nearby rivers and streams, and they pumped dirt and soot into the air.

**Q. How did trappers and hunters endanger animals?**

**A.** As people invented more powerful guns and better animal traps, hunters and trappers were able to kill more of their prey. The killing sometimes got out of control. Some animals, such as the bison (or American buffalo), almost disappeared. Killing bison actually became a form of entertainment. People passing by on trains would shoot them for sport. By 1890, there were fewer than 500 bison left. A hundred years before that there had been 60 million of them.

**Q. What did early American farmers do to harm the land?**

**A.** Some early farmers in the Great Plains used poor farming practices. They used the same fields over and over and removed all the nutrients in the soil. They allowed cattle and sheep to graze too much in one area. In many places, they removed the native plants that kept the soil from wearing away. The farmers ruined the land and could not grow food there any more.

## Q. What is conservation?

**A.** *Conservation* is using our natural resources wisely. It means protecting our plants and animals. It means protecting our soil, water, and other resources that give us life. The term comes from two Latin words: *con,* which means "together," and *servare,* which means "to guard or keep." Conservation means working together to keep, or protect, our natural resources.

## Q. Who was Gifford Pinchot?

**A.** Gifford Pinchot was probably the first person to convince the United States government to practice conservation. He served under President Theodore Roosevelt as the head of the United States Forest Service in the early 1900s. He helped to convince President Roosevelt to protect our national parks and forests.

## Q. What were some of the early conservation efforts?

**A.** Early conservation efforts helped to protect animals that were in danger of dying out, or becoming *extinct*. In 1903, the first government wildlife refuge was established on Pelican Island, Florida. This provided a place for the brown pelican to live, safe from the people who hunted the bird for its feathers. In the early 1900s, many laws were passed to protect forests, animals, and land.

**Q. What was the first national park?**

**A.** People began to think that one way to protect some of our beautiful and unusual land would be to have the government own it. In 1872, Yellowstone became the first national park in the world. The government took over the land to keep its natural beauty safe from hunters, trappers, and people who wanted to tear down its trees to build mines. The National Park Service was formed in 1916 to run the national parks.

**Q. How many national parks are there today?**

**A.** Today, there are almost 50 national parks, as well as 250 other types of monuments or historical sites protected by the National Park Service. Our beautiful parks contain mountains, lakes, waterfalls, caves, canyons, and even glaciers, all saved from destruction and protected by the government.

**Q. Who was John Muir?**

**A.** John Muir was an early environmentalist who worked to have Yosemite, Sequoia, and Kings Canyon named as national parks. Muir wanted to stop people from destroying nature. He formed the Sierra Club, which worked to save the Sierra Nevada Mountains in California. Today, the Sierra Club still works to protect the environment.

## Q. Who was Rachel Carson?

**A.** Rachel Carson wrote a book in 1962 called *Silent Spring*. This book told how poisons that people used to kill unwanted insects were also killing other creatures that we needed in our world. Her book made people so upset that laws were passed to control the use of these poisons.

## Q. What is Earth Day?

**A.** Earth Day is a day set aside in April to celebrate our planet and to learn ways to make it a better place to live. People all over the world join together to become more aware of their environment. The first Earth Day was held on April 22, 1970. It was one of the largest demonstrations in history.

## Q. What kinds of activities are held on Earth Day?

**A.** Many people participate in Earth-awareness fairs held in their cities on Earth Day. They enjoy entertainment, see environmental displays and exhibits, and talk to local groups working to help our Earth. Other people spend Earth Day cleaning up litter, planting trees, and doing other things to help the Earth. Find out what activities your community has planned for the next Earth Day, or spend the day helping to clean up your neighborhood.

**Q. What agency of the government is in charge of protecting the environment?**

**A.** The Environmental Protection Agency, or EPA, was established in 1970 to help keep our Earth clean. It sets and enforces rules to protect the environment. The EPA also helps cities and states set up programs to fight pollution.

**Q. What are some of the environmental problems facing the world today?**

**A.** It is hard to pick up a newspaper without seeing articles about oil spills polluting our water, landfills overflowing with garbage, animals losing their homes when people clear land for new buildings, and blackouts resulting from energy shortages. We hear about acid rain, holes in the ozone layer, and global warming. Fortunately, we also hear about people who are working hard to help find solutions to the problems we face.

**Q. Why should we be concerned about these problems?**

**A.** This is the only planet we have. It is our responsibility to take care of it. We need to learn all we can, to be well informed about the problems that exist, and to take action that will make a difference.

13

# PLANTS & ANIMALS

**Q. What is the web of life?**

**A.** The *web of life* refers to the way all plants and animals depend on each other for survival. Every living thing on our planet is part of the web of life.  Each plant and animal has a job to do that helps to keep the balance of nature. All plants and animals are important to the web of life.

**Q. How do plants and animals depend on one another?**

**A.** Plants and animals are *interdependent*. This means they need one another for survival. When we breathe, we exhale carbon dioxide, which is a gas plants need to live. Plants give off oxygen, which we need to breathe. Living things depend on one another in many ways. See if you can think of some more.

**Q. Are there other examples of plants and animals depending on each other?**

**A.** Bees and flowers depend on each other. Bees gather nectar and pollen from the blossoms of flowers to eat, to feed their young, and to make honey. In turn, the bees help the flowers to reproduce. As a bee flies from flower to flower, pollen from one flower sticks to the bee's legs. Some of that pollen falls off on the next flower the bee visits. That flower will then produce seeds that make new plants.

## Q. What is a food chain?

**A.** A *food chain* is a series of organisms that feed on each other. In the process, energy passes from one living thing to another. Green plants take food from the ground. Herbivores, or plant-eating animals, eat the green plants. Then meat-eating animals, or carnivores, eat the plant-eaters. Some animals eat both plants and animals. They are called omnivores.

## Q. How does the food chain work?

**A.** Here is an example of how the food chain works. A grasshopper feasts on some green leaves. A nearby toad then eats the grasshopper. A snake slithers by and eats the toad. An eagle swoops down and eats the snake. Even though the eagle did not eat any green plants, its energy came from the green plants that the grasshopper ate.

## Q. What are decomposers?

**A.** *Decomposers* are mushrooms, insects, worms, and other organisms that feed on decaying plant and animal matter. They are an important part of the food chain. Decomposers break down the decaying matter so that plants can use it for food. They put important food back into the soil. This helps to keep a food supply available to plants.

## Q. What is a species?

**A.** A *species* is a group of living things that are alike in almost every way. Members of the same species look and act like each other. Farm pigs and warthogs are both swine, but they are different species. Poodles and cocker spaniels are both members of the dog family, but they are different species.

## Q. What happens if a species leaves the food chain?

**A.** If a species disappears from the food chain, all of the animals in the food chain can suffer. If one plant dies out, the animals that ate that plant must find other food. The insects that made their homes in that plant must find other homes. Any animals that ate those insects would be affected, too.

## Q. What else can happen when the food chain changes?

**A.** When something upsets the balance of the food chain, some plants or animals can multiply too rapidly. This growth can cause problems for other living things. For example, people in Asia kill over 200 million bullfrogs each year because they enjoy eating the frogs' legs. The bullfrogs eat mosquitoes. With so many bullfrogs being killed, too many mosquitoes survive. Mosquitoes carry a disease called malaria. Many people suffer from malaria in Asia because of this change in the food chain.

**Q. What is a habitat?**

**A.** The place where a plant or animal lives and grows is a *habitat*. A habitat provides food, space to live, air, water, and shelter. The ocean is the habitat of seaweed and fish. The desert is the habitat of cactuses and tortoises. Seaweed and fish could not live in the desert, and cactuses and tortoises could not survive in the ocean.

**Q. How can you protect a plant's habitat?**

**A.** Enjoy looking at the plants and flowers you find in nature but do not remove them. Keep in mind that the soil, rocks, and fallen branches around a plant are part of its habitat. If you pick a beautiful wildflower and take it home, it will die. If you leave it in its natural habitat, you can enjoy its beauty and it can still play its part in the web of life.

**Q. How can you protect an animal's habitat?**

**A.** If you come across an animal, bird, or insect, do not disturb it. Do not remove a bird's nest or purposely destroy an anthill. Remember these three important steps to enjoying nature: look, learn, and leave it alone.

**Q. Where do plants and animals live?**

**A.** Plants and animals live everywhere—on land, in the sky, and in the ocean. Plants and animals live in an environment just as humans do. They live in icy waters, hot deserts, grassy plains, woodlands, swamps, and oceans around the world.

**Q. What is the tundra?**

**A.** The *tundra* is a cold, dry place where trees cannot grow. Snow and ice cover the ground most of the time. Northern Europe, Canada, Alaska, Asia, and parts of Antarctica have tundra.

**Q. Why are there so few animals on the tundra?**

**A.** Few animals can live on the tundra because it is so cold and windy and there are not many plants. Some of the animals that live on the tundra are Arctic foxes, caribou, polar bears, reindeer, snow owls, and penguins.

**Q. Have people threatened the tundra in the past?**

**A.** When explorers and trappers first came to the Arctic tundra long ago, they hunted and killed many of its animals. Two bird species, the great auk and the Labrador duck, died out completely because of these explorers and trappers.

**Q. What threatens the tundra today?**

**A.** Some scientists who visited the Antarctic for research left trash and other waste behind. The threat of oil spills in the waters around the tundra is a danger to the food supply of the animals. Other forms of pollution could also destroy the tundra. Fortunately, people have recognized the importance of the tundra and are working to preserve it.

**Q. What is a desert?**

**A.** A *desert* is a hot, dry region that receives little rainfall, usually less than ten inches a year. Temperatures in the desert often get higher than 100°F. Once the sun sets, it can get cold quickly. The only plants that can grow in this heat and dryness are ones like cactuses and date palms that require very little water to survive. Deserts cover about one seventh of the Earth's land.

**Q. What kinds of animals live in the desert?**

**A.** Desert animals must be able to live in a very hot and dry place. Camels, coyotes, jackrabbits, lizards, mice, mule deer, scorpions, and snakes are animals that survive in deserts around the world.

**Q. What threatens the desert habitat?**

**A.** More and more people are moving to the desert. Towns, farms, and roads are taking over more and more of the land. People destroy the plant life when they drive dune buggies, jeeps, and motorcycles across the desert. Also, ranchers often let their cattle and sheep graze on desert grasses. If the animals eat the grass faster than it can grow, the grass may not grow back again. Collectors take cactus plants from the desert. As a result, some varieties of cactus disappear.

21

**Q. What are grasslands?**

**A.** *Grasslands* are open, grassy plains that have a few trees scattered here and there. Grasslands have hot summers and cold winters. The prairies, found in midwestern states like Iowa and Kansas, are grasslands. Africa and Australia also have many huge grasslands.

**Q. What animals live on grasslands?**

**A.** Large animals such as the elephant, giraffe, hippopotamus, rhinoceros, lion, and zebra live in African grassland areas. The kangaroo lives on the grasslands of Australia. The prairie dog, the coyote, and the jackrabbit are some of the more familiar grassland animals of North America. Cows and sheep graze on grasslands around the world.

**Q. What affects the grassland habitat?**

**A.** Poor farming practices can hurt the grasslands. If sheep and cattle graze in one place for too long, they will destroy all of the grass. Without any plants to cover the ground, wind and rain can carry away the soil, and no new vegetation can grow. Hunters in the African grasslands kill animals such as the hyena and the elephant. Many of these animals are in danger of becoming extinct.

**Q. What are deciduous forests?**

**A.** *Deciduous forests* are homes to trees such as oak, maple, and beech. Deciduous trees shed their leaves once a year. Wildflowers that bloom in the spring grow in these forests. Deciduous forests have warm summers and cold winters. Many animals make their homes in deciduous forests. Bears, birds, raccoons, and squirrels all find food and shelter there.

**Q. What are coniferous forests?**

**A.** Conifers, or evergreen trees such as spruce and pine, grow in *coniferous forests*. Most conifers have needles instead of leaves. They do not shed their needles in the fall. Animals such as deer and wolves make coniferous forests their homes. These forests are cold most of the time. They receive much less sunshine than deciduous forests.

**Q. What has happened to many of the forests of the world?**

**A.** Forests once covered much of the world. Today, many of these forests are no longer standing. People destroyed them to clear the land for farms and cities. Pollution has also affected forests. It changes the soil so that it does not provide the proper food for trees.

**Q. What is deforestation?**

**A.** *Deforestation* means destroying a forest by cutting down or burning the trees. Deforestation destroys the plants and trees that provide food and homes for many animals. It also affects the air that we breathe because trees produce much of our oxygen.

**Q. How does deforestation lead to soil erosion?**

**A.** When people cut down large areas of trees, they also remove the plant roots that hold the soil in place. Rain and wind storms can then wear away the exposed soil, and no new plants can grow on the land.

**Q. How does deforestation affect the weather?**

**A.** Trees take a gas called carbon dioxide out of the air. If the trees are gone, the carbon dioxide stays in the air. This carbon dioxide traps heat near the Earth, so temperatures all over the world become higher.

**Q. What can you do to help save trees?**

**A.** If your family buys a Christmas tree, talk about getting a live tree that comes in a pot instead of one you throw away. When the holidays are over, plant the tree in your backyard. You can also plant a tree in the spring. If you don't have space in your yard, consider donating a tree to your school.

**Q. What is a tropical rain forest?**

**A.** A *tropical rain forest* gets at least 100 inches of rain a year. Tropical rain forests are very warm and very wet. They provide homes for a great many different plants and animals.

**Q. What kind of animals live in the tropical rain forest?**

**A.** Tropical rain forests are home to anteaters, frogs, flying squirrels, monkeys, snakes, and many, many insects and birds. The world's tropical rain forests contain about one half of all the plant and animal species on Earth.

**Q. Where are the tropical rain forests located?**

**A.** The rain forests are found close to the equator in parts of South America, Central America, Southeast Asia, and Africa. The largest tropical rain forest is the Amazon rain forest in South America.

**Q. What makes a rain forest so unique?**

**A.** Rain forests are different from other habitats because small sections of the rain forest can be completely different from sections right next to them. A few square miles of rain forest can be home to plant and animal species that live nowhere else on Earth.

**Q. What is the top layer of the rain forest?**

**A.** The rain forest has several different layers, and each layer has its own plants and animals. The top layer of the rain forest is the *emergent layer*. It contains very tall trees. Some of these trees grow taller than 160 feet. Butterflies and birds of prey such as eagles live in this level of the rain forest.

**Q. What is the rain forest canopy?**

**A.** The *canopy* rises about 100 to 130 feet above the ground of the tropical rain forest. It is very thick with vines and trees. It gets a lot of sunshine. Most of the plants and animals in the rain forest live in the canopy. Animals such as gibbons, lemurs, toucans, and parrots make their homes here. The tops, or crowns, of the trees in the canopy do not usually touch each other.

**Q. How do the spaces between the trees' crowns help protect the rain forest?**

**A.** Tropical storms occur often in the rain forest. The spaces between the crowns of the trees help to keep the trees safe from damage during storms by letting the wind blow through them. The spaces also keep caterpillars from going from one tree to another and eating all the leaves.

**Q. What is the understory?**

**A.** The layer beneath the canopy is called the *understory*. The bushes, shrubs, and trees there grow about 50 to 80 feet above the ground. The plants do not grow as tall in this layer because not as much sun reaches them. The thick canopy above the understory blocks a lot of the sun's rays. Bats, birds, and cats called ocelots live here.

**Q. What is the bottom layer of the rain forest called?**

**A.** The bottom layer of the rain forest is called the *forest floor*. Almost no direct sunlight reaches the forest floor. It is usually bare except for decaying plants and leaves and ferns, mosses, and other plants that don't need much sun. Beetles, spiders, tapirs, termites, and flightless birds live on the forest floor.

**Q. What animals are most numerous in the tropical rain forests?**

**A.** The rain forest has more insects than any other kind of animal. There are so many insect species that no one has been able to count them all. Scientists believe there are millions of different kinds of insects in our world's tropical rain forests. In just one square mile of African rain forest, over 300 different kinds of butterflies have been counted!

**Q. Do people live in the rain forests?**

**A.** There are many tribes of people who live in rain forests around the world. These people have learned a lot about the plants and animals that live in the rain forest. They know which plants and seeds in the forest can be good sources of food. They know how to use the plants of the rain forest for medicines.

**Q. How do rain forest plants help to treat diseases?**

**A.** About 25 percent of the drugs prescribed by American doctors have ingredients that come from rain forest plants. About 70 percent of the plants used to treat cancer grow *only* in the rain forest. Quinine is a cure for malaria. It comes from the bark of a South American rain forest tree. Ipecac can help someone who has swallowed poison. It comes from the rain forests of Brazil.

**Q. What foods come from the tropical rain forests?**

**A.** Nuts are one of the most common foods grown in the rain forest. Other rain forest foods include bananas, chocolate, cinnamon, coffee, tea, and vanilla. Many of the foods we grow on farms first grew in tropical rain forests. Some examples of these foods are oranges, rice, and sweet potatoes.

**Q. How do tropical rain forests help our air and water?**

**A.** The many plants in rain forests take carbon dioxide from the air and put oxygen back into the air. The tropical rain forests actually produce about 40 percent of the world's oxygen. Also, the rain forest trees play an important part in the Earth's water cycle by releasing water vapor into the air from their leaves. This water vapor eventually becomes rain. This affects rainfall and weather around the world.

**Q. How else do the rain forests affect our climate?**

**A.** Carbon dioxide is a gas that can keep heat from escaping the Earth. All trees take carbon dioxide from the air. Because rain forests have so many trees, they help to keep temperatures normal all over the world.

**Q. How do rain forests affect farming?**

**A.** Rain forests help to prevent soil erosion. The roots of trees in the rain forest absorb water and help prevent flooding. Floods can wash away the topsoil used for farming in areas near the rain forest.

CARBON DIOXIDE

OXYGEN

**Q. What problems do our tropical rain forests face?**

**A.** In the last 30 years, people have destroyed more than 40 percent of the world's rain forests. Much of the wood used in the United States comes from rain forests. Americans use this wood for such things as building houses and making paper.

**Q. Why else do people cut down the rain forests?**

**A.** In rain forest countries, people also cut down the trees to make pastures for cattle and to create farmland. Often the land supports the cattle and crops for only a few years. They clear the forest by using a method called slash and burn.

**Q. What does slash and burn mean?**

**A.** *Slash and burn* is a way of clearing rain forest trees. People cut down all of the trees in an area, take away or use the ones they want, and burn the rest. Native tribes used this way of clearing trees when they needed new farmland.

**Q. Do slash and burn methods hurt the rain forest today?**

**A.** Today, loggers and ranchers also use the slash and burn method to clear rain forests. Unlike the native tribes, though, they clear huge areas of rain forest land in a very short time. They pollute the air with their machines and with the smoke from the burning trees. They also destroy the rain forest habitat and all of the things it has to offer.

**Q. How fast are the rain forests disappearing?**

**A.** About 27 million acres of our tropical rain forests disappear each year. That means that every second, we destroy enough rain forest to cover a football field. If we continue to destroy them at this rate, there may not be any rain forests left in our world 50 years from now.

**Q. What is being done to help save the rain forests?**

**A.** Some countries set aside large areas of rain forest as natural reserves. In other countries, governments are studying new ways of logging and of replanting rain forest lands that people have destroyed. People have started organizations all over the world just to help save the rain forests.

**Q. What can you do to help save the rain forests?**

**A.** Look for other people in your community who are already working to save the rain forests. Sometimes you can find articles in your local newspaper about these groups and the work they are doing. You can also find lists of national organizations that are working to save the rain forests. Contact them to see how you can help and get involved.

**Q. Did you know that people raise beef cattle in the tropical rain forests?**

**A.** Ranchers have cleared large areas of rain forest land to raise cattle. The cattle on the ranches are raised for beef. Very often, fast food restaurants use beef from tropical rain forest lands in the food they sell.

**Q. Should you avoid buying rain forest products?**

**A.** Ask your mom or dad not to buy things made from wood taken from the rain forest. This includes furniture and other products made of rosewood, teak, and mahogany. Before you eat in a fast food restaurant, find out if the beef for the hamburgers comes from a tropical rain forest. Tell the manager of the restaurant about your concerns, or write a letter to the company that owns the restaurant.

**Q. What can you do at school to help the rain forests?**

**A.** Check out books from the library so you can read and learn more about the animals and plants that live in the rain forest. Get together with your friends and organize a rain forest club at your school. Ask your teacher and principal for their help. Plan fund-raising activities to help collect money. Donate the money you raise to organizations working to save the rain forests.

35

**Q. What are wetlands?**

**A.** *Wetlands* are low-lying areas filled with moisture. Examples of wetlands are bogs, deltas, lakes, marshes, ponds, and swamps. Wetlands cover about six percent of the Earth's land, and almost every country has them.

**Q. What kinds of animals can we find in wetlands?**

**A.** Wetlands are home to animals such as alligators, crayfish, and wading birds like cranes and herons. Ducks and other shore birds live in the wetlands. So do animals like the moose, the mink, and the muskrat.

**Q. What has happened to many of our wetlands?**

**A.** Of the 213 million acres of wetlands that once dotted the United States, less than half remain. People drained many wetland areas to make room for shopping centers and other buildings.

**Q. Why are wetlands important?**

**A.** Wetlands are important because they help prevent flooding and erosion. They hold and store water for long periods of time. Some plants that grow in wetlands are able to remove pollutants from the water. Wetlands are an important home to some unusual plants and animals.

**Q. What animals live in the ocean?**

**A.** Animals of many different sizes live in our oceans. Some are so tiny they can only be seen under a microscope. Others, like the blue whale, are huge. In fact, the blue whale can grow to be 97 feet long. Lobsters, squid, fish, penguins, and many other creatures also depend on the ocean.

**Q. Why are dolphins in danger?**

**A.** Dolphins often swim with yellowfin tuna. People catch the yellowfin tuna for food. They chase the dolphins and the tuna with speedboats until the animals become tired and confused. Then giant nets almost a mile long scoop them up. Any dolphins that get caught in the nets die. Over six million dolphins have died this way over the past 30 years.

**Q. What can you do to help save the dolphins?**

**A.** You can write letters to tuna companies and ask them to stop catching dolphins in their nets. You can also write to Congress. Ask them to help pass laws that will stop the killing of dolphins. Some tuna companies now use methods that do not endanger dolphins. Ask your mom or dad to buy only those brands of tuna. You can tell which brands to buy by reading the label on the can.

## Q. How does pollution affect marine life?

**A.** People dump hazardous materials into the ocean to get rid of them. Sewage and wastes from factories and cities can also reach the ocean. This pollution is very harmful. It can kill the plants and animals that make the ocean their home.

## Q. How can six-pack rings hurt marine animals?

**A.** Soda cans often come in plastic rings that make the cans easier to carry. These plastic rings are a danger to animals if they end up in our oceans, rivers, or lakes. Fish and birds sometimes get their beaks or necks caught in the rings. When this happens, they can choke or starve to death. If your family cuts the rings open before throwing them away, the animals will be safe.

## Q. What other trash can hurt marine animals?

**A.** When trash ends up in the water, it can hurt the animals that live there. Plastic shopping bags floating on the water can be mistaken for jellyfish. Sea animals that feed on jellyfish have died trying to eat these bags. Fishing lines that have been thrown away can trap fish and other sea life in their tangles. Ropes, cans, and glass can all be a hazard to the creatures that live in our waters.

**Q. How do people destroy natural habitats?**

**A.** People destroy the habitats of plants and animals by clearing land for roads, farms, or towns. People also create pollution that ruins our land and water and destroys the habitats of plants and animals. Animals must find new homes when these things happen. Sometimes they cannot find a place with a suitable environment, and the species dies out.

**Q. How do collectors endanger wildlife?**

**A.** Some people collect unusual plants and animals as a hobby. If these plants or animals are in danger of dying out, collectors can lower the already small populations of these species. This is a special danger for many species of birds, butterflies, cactuses, and orchids.

**Q. Are animals ever sold or transported illegally?**

**A.** Many countries have laws that make it illegal to take out or bring in certain animals. These laws keep people from removing the animals from their natural homes. But some greedy people smuggle animals such as parrots and tropical fish in order to sell them. Many of these animals die while they are being captured or moved.

**Q. Why is it important to protect plants and animals?**

**A.** Each and every living thing is an important part of the Earth. If one creature disappears, it can affect other plants and animals or even the whole environment. Also, we can learn from plants and animals by studying them. Sometimes this learning can lead to important discoveries like cures for diseases. We must also care for our plants and animals so we can preserve and enjoy their beauty.

**Q. How did early settlers endanger our wildlife?**

**A.** Long ago, settlers brought plants and animals with them when they came to a new land. Often, the new plants and animals took over or changed the existing web of life. When people came to the Galápagos Islands, rats from the explorers' ships came ashore and ate Galápagos turtle eggs. With this new threat, the turtle population almost disappeared.

**Q. Do hunters and trappers endanger animals?**

**A.** Hunters and trappers have killed large numbers of animals to make items such as blankets, coats, and jewelry. They hunt hawksbill turtles for their shells. They hunt elephants, walruses, and rhinos for their tusks or horns. They hunt jaguars, leopards, and seals for their furs.

**Q. What is a rare species?**

**A.** A *rare species* is a plant or animal that is uncommon. Often, governments protect rare species by making it illegal to disturb them. The torrey pine tree of California is one rare species. The Devil's Hole pupfish, found only in one small pool in Nevada, is another.

**Q. What is a threatened species?**

**A.** A *threatened species* is a plant or animal that faces some danger of dying out. The chimpanzee, the Guadalupe fur seal, the Utah prairie dog, and the mountain golden heather are all threatened species. The Arctic peregrine falcon is one threatened species that has increased its population after receiving protection. Maybe someday it will no longer be a threatened species.

**Q. What is an endangered species?**

**A.** An *endangered species* is one that is in extreme danger of dying out and disappearing. Endangered species receive special protection to save them from becoming extinct. The American peregrine falcon is an endangered species. Like the Arctic peregrine falcon, it has increased its population in recent years because of the protection it has received. Maybe one day it will be considered threatened instead of endangered.

*AMERICAN PEREGRINE FALCON*

*TORREY PINE TREE*

*UTAH PRAIRIE DOG*

45

KOMODO DRAGON

GIANT ARMADILLO

WEST AFRICAN OSTRICH

HAWKSBILL SEA TURTLE

TIGER

*GIANT KANGAROO RAT*

*SHORT-TAILED ALBATROSS*

*CALIFORNIA CONDOR*

**Q. What are some of the mammals on the endangered species list?**

**A.** Some of the mammals on the endangered list are the black rhinoceros, the blue whale, the giant armadillo, the giant kangaroo rat, the giant panda, the gorilla, the gray wolf, and the tiger.

**Q. What are some of the birds on the endangered species list?**

**A.** Some of the birds on the endangered list are the bald eagle, the brown pelican, the California condor, the indigo macaw, the oriental white stork, the short-tailed albatross, the thick-billed parrot, the West African ostrich, and the whooping crane.

**Q. What are some of the reptiles on the endangered species list?**

*SMALL WHORLED POGONIA ORCHID*

**A.** Some of the reptiles on the endangered list are the Alabama red-bellied turtle, the blunt-nosed leopard lizard, the Fiji banded iguana, the hawksbill sea turtle, the Indian python, and the Komodo Island monitor (also known as the Komodo dragon).

**Q. What are some of the plants on the endangered species list?**

**A.** Endangered plants include the Brady pincushion cactus, the green pitcher-plant, the scrub mint, and the small whorled pogonia orchid.

*GREEN PITCHER-PLANT*

45

MOA

GREAT AUK

IVORY-BILLED
WOODPECKER

PASSENGER
PIGEON

DODO

**Q. What does the term extinct mean?**

**A.** When an animal or a plant is *extinct*, it means there are no more of them. Every one of its kind has died, and there will never be any more. Sometimes it is hard to know if a species becomes extinct. The ivory-billed woodpecker is probably extinct, because no one has seen one for a long time. But no one knows for sure if every ivory-billed woodpecker has died.

**Q. What happened to the passenger pigeon?**

**A.** There were once so many passenger pigeons that people hunted them easily as they flew in huge numbers across the sky. But too many were hunted. Many of the trees the passenger pigeons lived in were cut down to build houses. Each female pigeon laid only one egg a year, so few babies were born to replace the many that died. In 1914, the last passenger pigeon died in the Cincinnati Zoo.

**Q. What other animals have become extinct?**

**A.** Some of the animals that are now extinct include the great auk, the dodo, the moa, the Labrador duck, and the quagga. You will never see them in their natural habitats. You will never visit them in zoos. But you can read about them and learn from them.

WHOOPING CRANE

GIANT PANDA

ALLIGATOR

**Q. What happened to save the whooping crane?**

**A.** In the 1940s, the world had less than 20 whooping cranes left. Scientists helped to save whooping cranes by protecting their eggs. Some of the eggs were given to another kind of bird, the sandhill crane, to hatch as its own. Today, there are over 150 whooping cranes alive. They may be saved from extinction.

**Q. What is being done to save the giant panda?**

**A.** The giant panda lives in China and eats bamboo, a type of grass that can grow as tall as a tree. People cleared many of the bamboo forests in China for homes and rice farms, destroying the pandas' homes. Also, people hunted the panda for its warm fur. Today, pandas and their habitats are protected. People are trying to save the giant panda from extinction.

**Q. How did we save the alligators?**

**A.** Not too long ago, people bought shoes, belts, purses, and wallets made of alligator skins. These items were so popular that alligators were in danger of dying out. They were named as an endangered species in 1967. Since then, alligators have increased in numbers.

**Q.  How are whales endangered?**

**A.**  People have hunted whales for centuries. People use whales as a source of food, and they use whale fat, or blubber, to make soap, glue, candles, perfumes, and fuel for lamps. To protect the whales, some countries made it illegal to kill them. Unfortunately, other countries continue to hunt whales. Many species of whales remain on the endangered list.

**Q.  What were elephant tusks used for?**

**A.**  Elephant tusks are made of ivory. People made jewelry, works of art, piano keys, and billiard balls from elephant tusks. Thousands and thousands of elephants died so people could have their tusks. Many governments no longer allow people to bring ivory into the country.

**Q.  What can you do to help protect endangered plants and animals?**

**A.**  One thing you can do is to know which products come from plants and animals that are on the endangered list. Tell your parents about things that come from endangered species. Ask them not to buy or use these products. This is one way of showing you care.

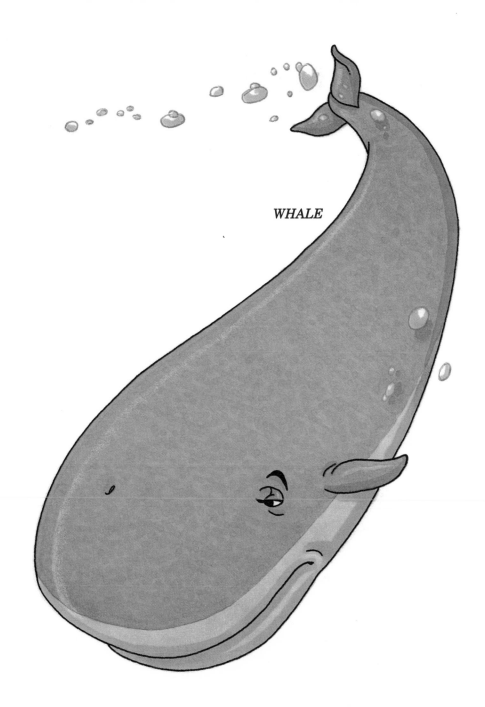

*WHALE*

*ELEPHANT*

**Q. How do zoos help protect animals?**

**A.** Zoos give homes to some animals that can no longer survive in the wild. The California condor is a bird that is in danger of dying out. There are only 25 California condors alive today. All of them live in zoos. Some zoos try to help the birds have babies to increase their population. Maybe someday California condors will be able to live in the wild again.

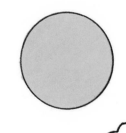

**Q. How can you adopt an animal?**

**A.** Many zoos have programs that let you adopt an animal. When you adopt an animal, it stays in the zoo to live. You make a donation that goes toward feeding and taking care of the animal. You might want to contact your zoo to see if they have a program you can join. Also, some environmental groups have programs that let you adopt animals in the wild.

**Q. How are plants and animals protected?**

**A.** Throughout the world, protected areas are established to help save wild animals and plants from becoming endangered. In these protected areas, plants and animals have a better chance of survival. There are more than 1,200 national parks, wildlife preserves, and areas around the world that people have set aside to protect plants and animals. People also pass laws that make it illegal to collect certain species, to hunt them, or to disturb their homes.

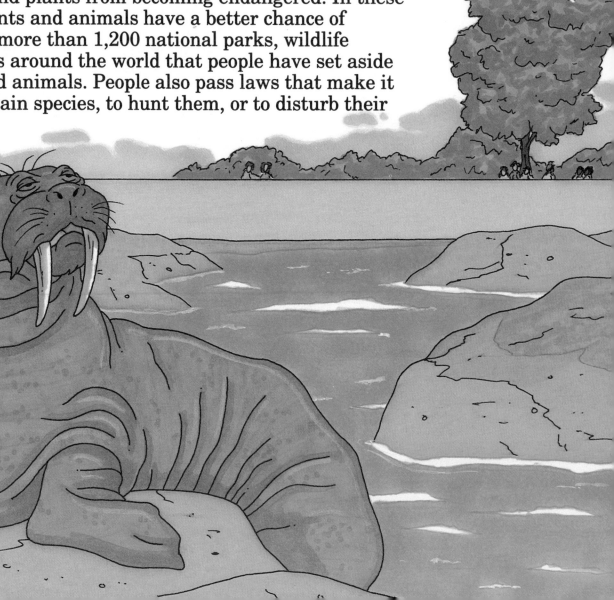

**Q. How can you do something nice for birds?**

**A.** Put a bird feeder in your backyard. Choose a spot outside to hang your feeder where birds will be safe from cats or other animals. You can also put a birdbath in your yard for birds to use. Have fun watching the different kinds of birds that come to your yard. Find a book about birds and see if you can identify your visitors.

**Q. How can you reuse a milk carton to make a bird feeder?**

**A.** First, get permission from mom or dad to do this project. Wash and dry an empty half-gallon milk carton. Cut windows on two facing sides, and cut a small hole below each window. Push a stick through the small holes to make a perch for the birds. Put birdseed in the bottom of your feeder. Use a paper clip or a bit of wire to hang the feeder outside.

**Q. How else can you do your share to help wildlife?**

**A.** Have respect and concern for the plants and animals that share this planet with you. Read and learn all you can about them. Be aware of the dangers that face many animals on Earth. Share what you learn with your family and friends. Talk about ways you can work together to help make a difference.

51

# WATER

## Q. What is water?

**A.** *Water* is the most common substance on the Earth. Every living thing contains water. The chemical symbol for water is $H_2O$. The symbol says that when two hydrogen (H) atoms join with one oxygen (O) atom, they form water. Water is the only thing on Earth that naturally occurs in three different forms.

## Q. What forms can water take?

**A.** Water can be a liquid, such as the water that comes out of your faucet. Water can be a solid, as in a block of ice. Water can be a gas, such as the steam or vapor you see when water boils.

## Q. Why is water important?

**A.** People, animals, and plants all need water to survive. Water helps you digest the food you eat and keeps you cool. Animals need water, too. Some, such as the camel, live in places where water is scarce. Others, such as dolphins and lobsters, actually make their homes in water. Water is an important part of the weather when it forms cooling rains and misty ocean breezes. There would be no life without water.

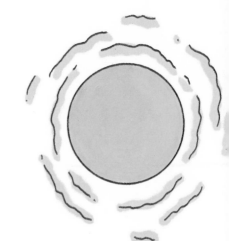

**Q. Why do plants need water?**

**A.** Water helps plants to make food for their survival. Water travels through the plants' roots and carries important minerals from the soil to the leaves. Water also helps plants to stand up straight. If plants don't get enough water, they will begin to wilt and droop.

**Q. How long can a person live without water?**

**A.** A person can live without food for over a month. But a person can only live for about a week without water. To stay healthy, a typical adult needs more than two quarts of water each day. You get water from the things you eat as well as from the things you drink. If the idea that food contains water surprises you, think of some of the juicy foods you enjoy eating. An ear of corn is 70 percent water, an apple is over 80 percent water, and tomatoes and watermelon are more than 90 percent water!

**Q. How much water is in living things?**

**A.** Every living thing has water in it. Flowers, trees, birds, snakes, insects, fish, whales, and you all contain water. The human body contains about 65 percent water.

**Q. How much of the Earth has water on it?**

**A.** Water is found almost everywhere on Earth. It is in our rivers, lakes, streams, and oceans. It is even in the ground and in the air we breathe. Water covers more than 70 percent of the Earth's surface.

**Q. How much of the Earth's water can we use?**

**A.** We can use very little of the Earth's water. Only about three percent of the Earth's water is fresh water. The rest is salt water found in our oceans and seas. Most of the fresh water is not usable because it is frozen in glaciers and ice caps. Less than one percent of all the water on Earth is usable to us.

**Q. Does the amount of water on the Earth ever change?**

**A.** No. We have the same amount of water we have always had. Although we drink, spill, and throw away water all the time, the Earth has a natural system called a water cycle that produces fresh rainwater over and over again.

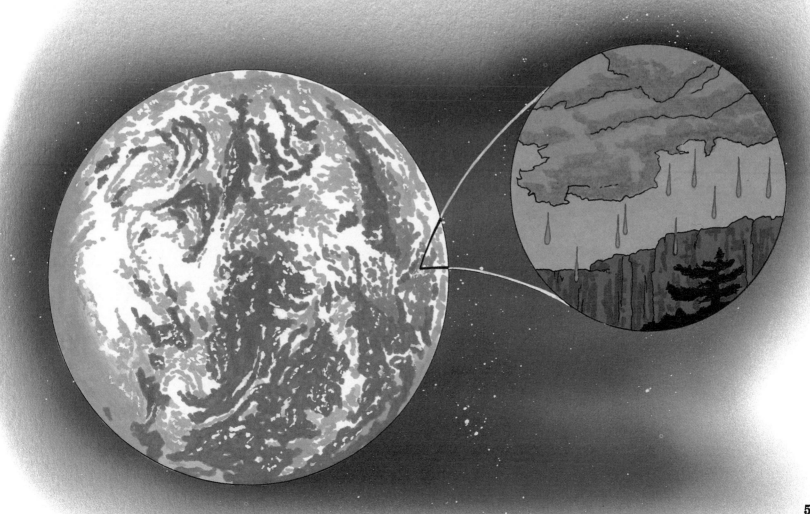

## Q. What is a water cycle?

**A.** A *water cycle* is a natural process that starts when water evaporates from oceans, lakes, rivers, and streams. In the atmosphere, the water collects as vapor to form clouds, then condenses to form drops, and falls to the ground as precipitation such as rain or snow. The precipitation ends up in rivers, lakes, oceans, and streams, and the process starts over. This is a water cycle.

## Q. What is evaporation?

**A.** *Evaporation* occurs when water enters the air in the form of a gas. To see evaporation at work, try this simple experiment. Ask your parents for permission to leave a small amount of water in an uncovered dish for two or three days. Check the water level in the dish each day. You'll find less and less water each time. The water is leaving the dish and entering the air through the process of evaporation.

## Q. What is condensation?

**A.** *Condensation* occurs when water vapor in the air becomes cool. When its temperature drops, the water vapor turns into drops of liquid water. Condensation forms the beads of water, or dew, on your grass in the morning.

## Q. What is precipitation?

**A.** *Precipitation* is water that falls from the sky. It can be in the form of a thunder shower, a snowy blizzard, pounding hail, or icy sleet.

*EVAPORATION*          *PRECIPITATION*

## Q. What is groundwater?

A. *Groundwater* is water that flows under the ground. Today, groundwater provides much of the water we use every day at home, school, work, and play. The rest of our water comes from rivers, lakes, and streams. Aqueducts carry water from rivers and other places where it is plentiful to places where it is needed.

## Q. What is an aqueduct?

A. An *aqueduct* is a channel that is built to carry water from where it is to where it is needed. This word comes from two Latin words—*aqua,* meaning "water," and *ducere,* meaning "to lead". The Romans built a system of aqueducts more than 2,000 years ago. The longest modern aqueduct is in California. This aqueduct is 826 miles long, which is almost the distance between New York and Atlanta!

## Q. What is a reservoir?

A. A *reservoir* is a place that stores water for future use. Some reservoirs are built by people, such as a dam or a rain barrel, and others are natural, such as lakes and springs. The water in a reservoir comes from falling rain and melting snow.

**Q. How much rain falls in the United States?**

**A.** The United States as a whole gets plenty of rain each year, although not all areas of the country get the same amount. The United States gets an average of about 30 inches of rainfall a year. Look in an almanac or encyclopedia to find the average rainfall in your state.

**Q. Why are there water shortages?**

**A.** Many things can cause water shortages. Some places on the Earth naturally do not have much water. Sometimes an area will have a long period with little or no rainfall, called a drought, that can cause a shortage. Some water shortages happen because people do not take care of the water they have.

**Q. Why are there floods?**

**A.** Most floods happen when too much rain falls in a short time. Floods can occur anywhere—on farmlands, in cities, in deserts, or on mountains. When rain hits the ground, some of the water soaks into the soil and some runs off into nearby streams and creeks. When the soil is filled with water, the rainfall runs off the surface of the soil. If too much water flows into rivers, they can overflow their banks, causing a flood.

**Q. What are some of the ways we use water?**

**A.** We use water for drinking, cleaning, cooking, flushing toilets, bathing, generating power, fighting fires, irrigating farms, doing laundry, and washing dishes. Water is used to keep car engines from overheating. Barges and ships travel on rivers and oceans to transport heavy and bulky things like machinery and oil.

**Q. How do we use water to have fun?**

**A.** Water is important for many of the things we enjoy in our spare time. We use it for activities such as swimming, skiing, snorkeling, fishing, and sailing. We use water when we go on water rides at amusement parks and when we run through a lawn sprinkler on a hot day.

**Q. How many times does your family use water in a day?**

**A.** For one day, keep track of all the times you and your family use water. Keep a piece of paper and a pencil with you throughout the day. Each time you use water for any reason, write down how you used it. Ask each member of your family to do the same. At the end of the day, get together and talk about all the ways your family uses water.

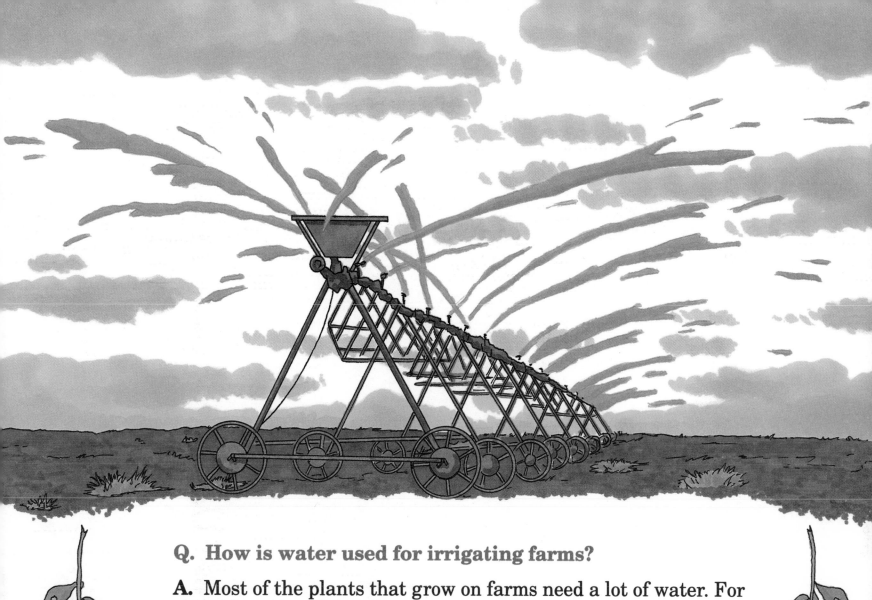

## Q. How is water used for irrigating farms?

**A.** Most of the plants that grow on farms need a lot of water. For example, 115 gallons of water are needed to grow enough wheat to make just one loaf of bread. When farmers irrigate their crops, they pipe water from rivers, lakes, or wells. Farmers in the United States use about 220 billion gallons of water a day for irrigation. This is enough water to fill a lake.

## Q. How do we use water to generate power?

**A.** We use water to produce electric power to run our factories and to light our homes and offices. Electric power stations burn coal or other fuel and use the heat to turn water into steam. The steam runs machines that make electricity.

## Q. How does industry use water?

**A.** Industry uses water in many ways. Besides using water to make steam for electric power, industry uses water to cool down hot metals, gases, and machinery. Industry uses water to make paper, steel, and glass and to make soft drinks, bubble gum, canned soups, and packaged meats. Factories in the United States use about 140 billion gallons of water daily.

**Q. What is water pollution?**

**A.** People cause water pollution when they dump wastes such as chemicals, metals, and oil into oceans, lakes, rivers, and other bodies of water. Water pollution is a serious problem in the United States. When we pollute water, it can look dirty and smell bad. Sometimes polluted water contains chemicals and germs that can make you sick. Green water has too many tiny plants called algae growing in it. When the algae die, they decompose and use up oxygen that animals need to survive. If the water has a shiny film on the surface, it could be an oil slick. Foam or suds in the water could come from detergents from homes or factories. If the water smells rotten, it might mean sewage has been dumped nearby. It is difficult to identify all polluted water by appearances, because sometimes polluted water shows *none* of these signs!

**Q. What are the main sources of water pollution?**

**A.** The main sources of water pollution are sewage, industry, and agriculture. Sewage is human wastes and water that has been used for bathing and cleaning clothes. Industry puts three to four times as many pollutants into water as all of our sewage systems do. Chemicals and other waste from farms also pollute our water.

**Q. How do agricultural wastes contribute to water pollution?**

**A.** Some farmers use chemical fertilizer to help their crops grow. They also use pesticides to kill pests such as insects and weeds. Rainwater can carry these chemicals from the farmland into streams. Animal wastes from farms also add to water pollution.

**Q. What are hazardous wastes?**

**A.** *Hazardous wastes* are leftover or unwanted materials that are harmful to living things when they are disposed of improperly. Many common products contain ingredients that are toxic, or poisonous. For example, motor oil is necessary to keep a car running smoothly. But if people dump used motor oil into the ground, it can seep into the groundwater and damage the water supply.

**Q. What is a toxic substance?**

**A.** A *toxic substance* is a chemical that may be a risk to your health or to the environment when it is made, used, distributed, or thrown away. For example, paint is not something you think of as a dangerous substance. But paints used to contain lead. When old lead paint begins to flake, small children sometimes eat the flakes. This could cause lead poisoning, which can be very dangerous.

**Q. What are some of the effects of toxic substances?**

**A.** Some toxic substances can cause dizziness and vomiting. They can cause changes in your behavior and make a difference in how alert you are. Some toxic substances even cause serious diseases such as cancer.

**Q. How do dangerous wastes get into our groundwater?**

**A.** When people dump toxic substances such as bug spray, nail polish remover, and household cleaning products in landfills, the chemicals in these products may seep through the soil into the groundwater. When people pour toxic substances such as paint, drain cleaners, and bleach down their bathroom or kitchen sinks, the chemicals in these products can leak into the groundwater.

**Q. How can you tell what products in your home may be toxic?**

**A.** Ask your parents for permission to read the labels on household cleaners in your home. Some will have words that tell you the product contains hazardous materials. Look for words such as *Caution, Danger, Poison, Warning, Harmful or fatal if swallowed, Flammable,* and *Keep out of reach of children.* Stay away from products that contain these warning words.

**Q. What are some products in your home that might contain hazardous ingredients?**

**A.** Common, everyday things in your home can contain hazardous ingredients. Things like furniture polish, drain cleaners, mothballs, oven cleaners, enamel or oil paints, pool chemicals, disinfectants, toilet cleaners, paint thinners, and bleach all contain hazardous ingredients.

**Q. What can you do about hazardous products?**

**A.** First, when you are in the supermarket with your mom or dad, read the labels on household cleaners. Ask your parents to buy products that contain few or no toxic substances. Encourage them to buy only what you and your family need and will use in a short time.

**Q. How can you dispose of hazardous wastes?**

**A.** You and your family can find out where to dispose of household chemicals such as paint and drain cleaners by contacting your local sanitation department. They will tell you where you can find approved community collection programs, landfills, or recycling centers for these toxic substances.

**Q. What is a detergent?**

**A.** A detergent is a cleansing agent. Most detergents your parents buy in the store are liquids or powders that dissolve in water. We use detergents to wash our clothes and dishes. Laundry detergents clean clothes by making the cloth fibers soak up water. Then dirt and oil can be lifted off the fabric and rinsed away. Dishwashing detergents clean by loosening the food and grease on dishes.

**Q. What are phosphates?**

**A.** Phosphates are chemicals that are added to some detergents to increase the amount of suds they produce and to make these suds last longer. Find the detergents your family uses at home. Read the labels to see if they contain any phosphates.

**Q. How do phosphates harm the environment?**

**A.** In very small amounts, phosphates are good for the environment. They help plants make food. But large amounts of phosphates in lakes and streams speed up the growth of tiny plants called algae. When algae plants thrive this way, they can block out sunlight and use up nutrients. When the algae die, they decompose and use up oxygen. This deprives other plants and animals that live nearby of the things they need to survive.

**Q. What are some of the effects of water pollution?**

**A.** Polluted water can kill plants and animals. Polluted water can make people very sick. Rivers and lakes can become so polluted that we can no longer use them for drinking, swimming, or boating.

**Q. What are people doing to stop water pollution?**

**A.** The United States government has passed laws that limit what people can dump into water. Many industries have stopped using waterways as a place to dump their wastes. Many cities are building treatment plants to help clean up sewage. Scientists are looking for new ways to reduce and solve the water pollution problem.

**Q. What can you do about water pollution?**

**A.** Show pride and respect for the rivers, lakes, beaches, streams, and ponds in your community. Talk to your teacher about adopting a waterway as a class project. Encourage your family to use products that do not contain hazardous ingredients or at least to learn how to safely dispose of the ones you do use. Read and learn more about water pollution and what you can do to help.

**Q. What is an oil slick?**

**A.** Sometimes offshore wells, leaky pipelines, or oil tankers will spill oil. Because oil does not mix with water, the oil forms a widespread film on top of the water. This floating film is called an *oil slick*.

**Q. How do oil spills affect our water?**

**A.** Oil spills are a serious danger. An oil spill can kill many water birds, fish, otters, turtles, and any other wildlife that runs into it. Spills can also wash up on land. This can ruin beaches and shoreline and threaten the plants and animals that live there. Oil spills are very difficult and expensive to clean up.

**Q. How do oil spills affect birds and animals?**

**A.** When oil spills occur, oil coats the feathers of birds. This removes the air layer that protects them from the cold. Being covered with oil also makes it hard for sea animals to swim. They are unable to dive for food or swim away from enemies. The oil can get into eggs laid at the water's edge and kill the baby animals inside. Fish can die because the oil clogs their gills and they can't breathe. Oil contaminates the food and water needed by the sea animals. Many creatures die when we spill oil in the water.

**Q. What famous oil spill happened in Alaska in 1989?**

**A.** An oil tanker, the Exxon *Valdez*, ran aground near Valdez, Alaska, on March 24, 1989. More than ten million gallons of oil spilled from its torn hull into Alaska's Prince William Sound.

**Q. What were some of the results of this oil spill?**

**A.** As a result of this spill, more than 33,000 seabirds, 980 otters, and 136 bald eagles died. Many volunteers worked day and night to save the wildlife. They cleaned many animals that would have died otherwise.

**Q. How are oil spills cleaned up?**

**A.** Workers make a ring of floating devices called booms around the oil spill to stop it from spreading. A pump then collects the oil that floats on the surface of the water. Sometimes clean-up crews use materials that absorb or soak up the oil. Detergents can also be used to break up oil spills. But detergents may harm marine life.

**Q. Is oil pollution caused only by accidents at sea?**

**A.** Oil pollution is not limited to accidents at sea. Cars need to have their oil changed regularly in order for them to run properly. Many people throw used motor oil down the drain or on the ground where it can contaminate the groundwater. One quart of motor oil can ruin 250,000 gallons of drinking water.

**Q. What is the proper way to dispose of motor oil?**

**A.** Ask your parents to be careful about the way they dispose of their used motor oil. They can take it to a gas station or special disposal facility. There, people will recycle the oil or dispose of it in a way that is safe for the environment.

**Q. What can you and your family do to help stop oil pollution?**

**A.** Learn more about how oil pollution affects our water and what businesses can do to prevent future oil spills. Write letters to politicians and to the people whose businesses cause oil spills and tell them how you feel. If we show companies that we care about the way they affect the environment, they will work hard to take better care of our world.

## Q. What is an acid?

**A.** An *acid* is a chemical compound that tastes sour or bitter and will dissolve in water. An acid can irritate your skin and eyes. Some acids are so strong they can actually dissolve rocks. The pH scale is used to describe the strength of an acid. This scale goes from 0, which means very acid, to 14, which means not acid at all, or alkaline.

## Q. What is an alkali?

**A.** An *alkali* is a chemical compound that is the opposite of an acid. By adding just the right amount of an alkali to an acid, it is possible for them to mix and become neutralized. This means the mixture is neither acid nor alkali.

## Q. How do you measure acidity?

**A.** To measure acidity yourself, buy some litmus paper and a color chart at a pet shop or pharmacy. Dip the litmus paper in three or four common, nontoxic liquids such as vinegar, lemon juice, milk, or dishwashing liquid. Compare the colors of the wet litmus strips to the color chart. This will tell you whether the liquids are acid, alkali, or neutral.

POLLUTANTS

EVAPORATION

ACID RAIN

## Q. What is acid rain?

**A.** People make *acid rain* by putting pollutants in the air. Each day, automobile exhaust pipes and chimneys from factories spew chemicals into the air. These chemicals become part of the rainwater in the clouds and form acids. When this acid rain falls, all the acids end up in our soil and in our lakes, rivers, and oceans.

## Q. How does acid rain damage structures?

**A.** Many of the statues, bridges, and buildings in our cities are made of limestone. Limestone reacts with the chemicals in the acid rain by dissolving. After being exposed to acid rain year after year, these structures can become pitted, weakened, and even destroyed.

## Q. How does acid rain harm the environment?

**A.** When acid rain soaks into the ground, it dissolves valuable minerals in the soil and carries them away. Acid rain also damages tree leaves, slows plant growth, and changes the streams and lakes into which it falls. It can destroy foods that fish eat and keep fish eggs from hatching.

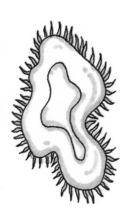

**Q. Is your water safe to drink?**

**A.** In most communities, the water is safe to drink. The United States has laws like the Safe Drinking Water Act to be sure that drinking water is safe. This law helps to set rules for the 240,000 public water systems in the United States. This law also helps to protect the water supply from pollution.

**Q. How can you test your water?**

**A.** If you and your family want to find out how safe the water in your home is, you can find the name and phone number of a testing service by looking under "Water" in the yellow pages of the telephone directory. They will test the water for metals, pesticides, and other impurities.

**Q. Why is water treated?**

**A.** When people and nature put things in our lakes and rivers, it makes the water dirty and impure. Tiny organisms that carry diseases can begin to grow. These organisms can make people sick. For these reasons, we treat water to make it safe for drinking, bathing, and washing. This happens at a water treatment plant.

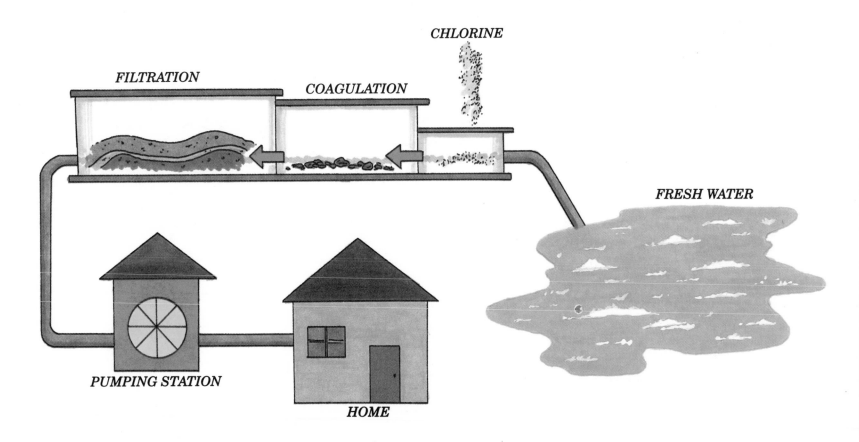

FILTRATION

COAGULATION

CHLORINE

FRESH WATER

PUMPING STATION

HOME

**Q. What happens at a water treatment plant?**

**A.** First, large items such as sticks, logs, plants, and fish are screened out and removed. Helpful chemicals are added to the water to remove impurities and to destroy any unpleasant tastes and odors. Then the water is mixed quickly to distribute the chemicals evenly.

**Q. What is coagulation?**

**A.** *Coagulation* is the next step in the water treatment process. The water and the chemical mixture are placed in a large basin. The chemicals cling to the impurities in the water, forming particles. This process is called coagulation. Larger particles settle to the bottom of the basin and are removed.

**Q. How is water filtered?**

**A.** The next step at the water treatment plant is *filtration*. The water is filtered through layers of sand, gravel, and hard coal to remove any other impurities. An additional filter may be used to remove toxic organisms.

**Q. Why is chlorine added to water?**

**A.** Chlorine is added to the water to prevent the formation of bacteria. This chlorine is carefully measured so that the smallest useful amount is used.

TREATMENT PLANT

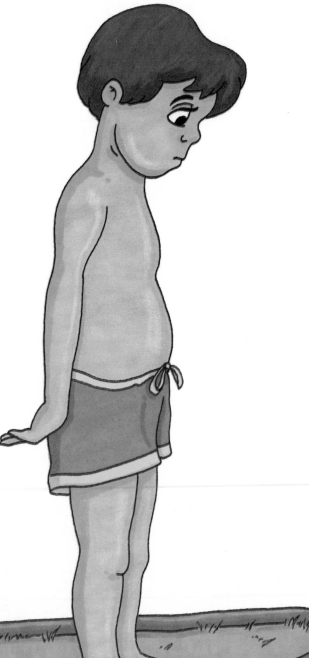

**Q. How does water get from the treatment center to your home or to factories?**

**A.** The water at the treatment plant is now ready for people to use. The water may be stored in a reservoir or tank. It travels in large pipes called mains to the areas where it is needed. The mains that carry water run under the streets in your community. Mains are connected to other smaller pipes. These pipes carry water to homes, offices, restaurants, shops, and other buildings.

**Q. What makes water travel through the mains?**

**A.** Water travels through the pipes because of pressure. Pumps use tremendous force or pressure to send the water to the mains. This keeps the water moving from pipes into your faucet so the water is there when you need it.

**Q. What happens when too many people use water at once?**

**A.** If a lot of people in your house use water at the same time, the demand for water may be too great. If your dad is doing laundry, your mom is in the shower, and you are outside filling your sister's wading pool with the hose, the water pressure might drop. Instead of a steady stream of water, you might have just a trickle.

**Q. What happens to your used water after it leaves your home?**

**A.** Your used water travels underground to a sewage treatment plant. Here, the water is cleaned and carried by pipes to streams, rivers, and lakes. It is then ready to go back to the water treatment plant and then to homes and factories for use again.

**Q. How does the water company know how much water you use?**

**A.** Most homes have water meters that measure the amount of water that is used. Someone from the water company comes out to read the meter on a regular basis. Water companies then send a bill for the water that you used.

**Q. Why is it important to save water?**

**A.** Water is an important natural resource. Although many places around the world have plenty of water, others have too little. Also, treating water and sending it to your home takes energy. When you save water, you also save energy and reduce pollution.

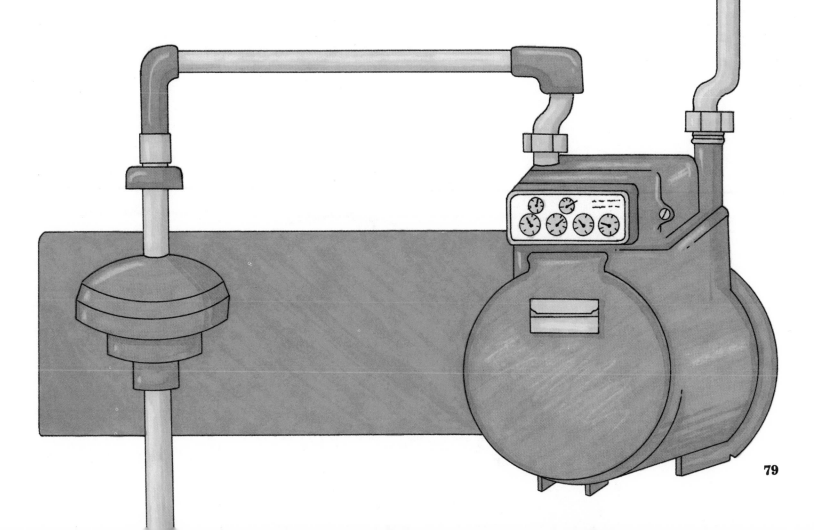

79

**Q. What activity in your home uses the most water?**

**A.** The largest single use of water in a home is toilet flushing. A toilet uses about six gallons of water for each flush. Keep track of the number of times you flush a toilet each day for one week. Multiply that figure by six to find out how many gallons of water you used to flush your toilet that week.

**Q. How can your toilet be a water-saver?**

**A.** You can reduce the amount of water your toilet uses. Reuse a plastic milk or juice jug. After you remove any labels, put small rocks in the jug to make it weigh more. Fill the jug with water and replace the cap. Ask your mom or dad to take the tank cover off your toilet and put your jug inside the tank. This takes up space in the tank where the water used for each flush is stored. Each time you flush, you will save one or two gallons of water.

**Q. How much water do other activities in the home use?**

**A.** A two-minute shower uses about 24 gallons of water while a ten-minute shower uses more than 100 gallons of water. An average bath uses more than 40 gallons of water. It takes up to ten gallons of water to wash the dishes and up to 30 gallons to run an automatic washing machine.

**Q. How can you save water when you bathe?**

**A.** If you take a bath, do not fill the bathtub with more water than you need. If you take a shower, cut down the amount of time you run the shower water. Use a three-minute egg timer and try to finish your shower before the time is up. When you shampoo your hair, turn the water off. Only turn it on again when you are ready to rinse the suds. Ask your parents to put a low-flow shower head in your shower.

**Q. What is a low-flow shower head?**

**A.** A low-flow shower head is a device that saves water. It will slow the water flow from 12 gallons to three gallons per minute. By using a low-flow shower head, your family can reduce the amount of water used in the shower by 75 percent.

**Q. How else can you save water in the bathroom?**

**A.** While you brush your teeth, turn the water off after you wet your toothbrush. Turn it on again when you are ready to rinse. By doing this, you can save about two gallons of water. Also, turn the water off while you wash your hands and face. Turn the water on again to rinse.

**Q. How can you save water in your yard?**

**A.** Keep a rain barrel or bucket in your backyard for collecting rainwater. The best place to put it is under a rain gutter where you can catch a lot of water at once. Use the water you collect on plants, shrubs, and trees around your house, or use it to wash your bike or the family car.

**Q. How can you tell how long you should turn on your sprinkler?**

**A.** An average lawn needs about one inch of water a week. Try this experiment. Place three empty cans around the area you plan to water. Put them at different distances from your sprinkler. Water your lawn. Use a plastic ruler to check the water levels in each can every five minutes. Write down how long it takes to get one inch of water in each can. Add the three times together and divide by three to get an average. This is how long you need to leave the sprinkler on.

**Q. What is a drip system?**

**A.** A drip system provides constant water for plants by dripping water into the soil. This means not as much water is wasted by evaporation. A drip system keeps the soil moist and loose. It can help cut your garden watering in half.

**Q. How can you save water in the kitchen?**

**A.** Put a bowl or pan in the sink to catch the cool water that runs while you are waiting for the water to turn hot. Use the water you collect on your plants. When you do the dishes, save water by soaking them in a sink full of water. Rinse them in the sink or a bowl of clean water instead of under running water. Add food scraps to a compost pile instead of using water to grind them up in an automatic garbage disposal.

**Q. How much water does a leaky faucet waste?**

**A.** A drip from a leaky faucet can waste more than 50 gallons of water a day. Fifty gallons is enough to flush a toilet eight times or wash the dishes by hand after five meals.

**Q. What can you do about leaky faucets?**

**A.** Check all of the faucets in your kitchen and bathrooms to see if any of them are leaking. If they are, put a bowl or small pail under the faucet to catch the drips before they go down the drain. Use the water to refill your pet's water bowl or to water plants around your house. Tell your mom or dad about the leaky faucet so they can fix it as soon as possible.

**Q. How can you learn more about water in your community?**

**A.** Talk with your mom or dad to learn more about where your community gets its water. Find out how much water your community uses. See if you can learn how your water is treated and disposed of. Your local water department can answer many of these questions and tell you where to get more information.

**Q. How can you save water when you are not at home?**

**A.** Practice saving water when you are visiting family and friends. Tell them about your methods of saving water at your house. When you go to a restaurant, ask them not to serve you water unless you are going to drink it. This way, you save drinking water and the water it takes to wash your glass afterward.

**Q. What else can you do to protect our existing water supplies?**

**A.** You can help keep our water clean by supporting stronger laws that forbid dumping poisonous chemicals and sewage into our lakes, rivers, and oceans. You can talk to friends, family, and teachers about ways to keep our water clean. You can read and learn more about what we can do to protect our water.

# LAND

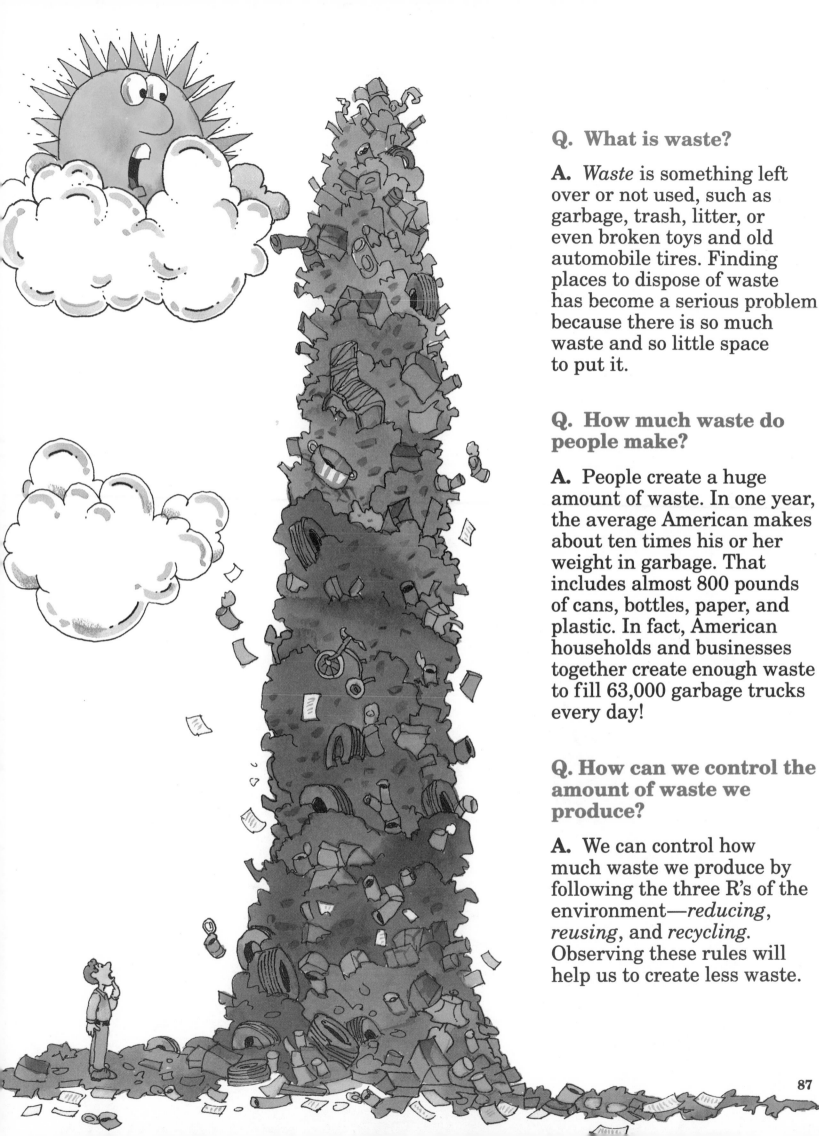

**Q. What is waste?**

**A.** *Waste* is something left over or not used, such as garbage, trash, litter, or even broken toys and old automobile tires. Finding places to dispose of waste has become a serious problem because there is so much waste and so little space to put it.

**Q. How much waste do people make?**

**A.** People create a huge amount of waste. In one year, the average American makes about ten times his or her weight in garbage. That includes almost 800 pounds of cans, bottles, paper, and plastic. In fact, American households and businesses together create enough waste to fill 63,000 garbage trucks every day!

**Q. How can we control the amount of waste we produce?**

**A.** We can control how much waste we produce by following the three R's of the environment—*reducing*, *reusing*, and *recycling*. Observing these rules will help us to create less waste.

87

## Q. What is reducing?

**A.** *Reducing* means using less. If we try to use fewer things that will produce trash, we will be taking the first step toward solving the waste problem.

## Q. How can you reduce what you use?

**A.** Choose things you can use again, such as cloth towels instead of paper towels. Make it a habit to ask yourself if you really need what you are about to use or buy. Doing without things you don't really need will help the environment.

## Q. What is reusing?

**A.** *Reusing* is taking items you would ordinarily throw away and finding ways to use them again. Many people reuse cardboard boxes, glass jars, grocery bags, cards, and envelopes.

## Q. What other items can you reuse?

**A.** You can save and reuse plastic bags by turning them inside out, rinsing them, and letting them dry. You can wrap a birthday present with the comic pages from the Sunday newspaper or with an old paper bag you have decorated. Or, you can reuse empty mayonnaise jars to hold a collection of pennies.

**Q. What is recycling?**

**A.** *Recycling* is processing waste so that we can use it again. Some of the things people recycle are aluminum, glass, paper, and plastic. When we recycle things, less trash finds its way into bulging garbage dumps. Recycling also uses less energy and natural resources than making new products.

**Q. What is precycling?**

**A.** *Precycling* means thinking about the waste a product will create before you buy it. When people precycle, they buy things in recyclable packages that won't end up as garbage. Sometimes precycled things are materials that have already been recycled, such as containers made of steel, paper, cardboard, aluminum, and glass.

**Q. How can you tell if something can be or has been recycled?**

**A.** Many companies are making products and packaging from recycled materials. They use a symbol of three arrows in the shape of a triangle to show that a product has been or can be recycled. On plastic containers, this triangle contains a number that indicates the type of plastic used to make the container.

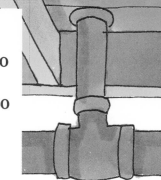

**Q. What are examples of recycling?**

**A.** Recycling is crushing glass bottles and melting them down to make new glass. It is turning paper back into pulp and making new paper from that pulp. Recycling is also shredding plastics to make filling for jackets you wear. Recycling is mixing grass cuttings with food scraps to make fertilizer for your garden.

**Q. What are the steps in the recycling process?**

**A.** The four recycling steps are collecting, sorting, reclaiming, and reusing. First, we collect recyclable materials such as paper, plastic, metal, and glass and take them to a recycling center. There they are sorted by type because each must be recycled in a different way. Then they go through a reclaiming process such as melting so that they are in a form we can use. Finally, the recycled materials are reused in new products.

**Q. What can you do to recycle?**

**A.** There are many ways you can recycle. At home, you can help your family to recycle. You can start a drive to collect newspapers, aluminum cans, and other recyclable materials at your school or in your neighborhood. You can encourage your friends and family to make recycling a habit.

**Q. What is curbside recycling?**

**A.** Many communities collect recyclable materials from the curbs in front of people's homes. People sort their plastic, glass, and paper trash into separate bins. Trucks pick up the bins and deliver them to recycling centers. Making it so easy encourages more people to recycle.

**Q. What steps can you take to prepare trash for curbside recycling?**

**A.** If you participate in a curbside recycling program, you can start by rinsing and crushing the aluminum cans you collect. Keep newspapers clean and dry, and if you store them outside, tie them in bundles or place them in paper bags to keep them from blowing away. Rinse out glass bottles and jars, and remove all bottle caps and rings.

**Q. How can you find out more about recycling in your community?**

**A.** Look in your telephone book to find the number of your community waste management office. Call and let them know you are interested in recycling. They can direct you to the closest recycling center and give you information about any other kinds of recycling done in your community.

**Q. What is litter?**

**A.** *Litter* is trash that has not been discarded properly. Litter is a soda can tossed on a sandy beach, a gum wrapper carelessly dropped on a playground, or a bag thrown from a car window.

**Q. Why is litter a problem?**

**A.** Litter takes away from the beauty of our environment. It is also unhealthy. Litter can make small animals sick if they eat the plastic from food packages. People and animals can cut themselves on broken bottles and sharp cans.

**Q. What can you do about litter?**

**A.** Organize a "litter day" at school. Get a group of friends together to pick up litter on the playground during recess. When collecting litter, wear protective gloves and be careful if you pick up anything sharp.

**Q. What happens to litter?**

**A.** Uncollected litter will remain on the ground until it breaks down into the soil or someone puts it into a trash container. Once the litter is in a trash container, it will go to a landfill, where your household garbage goes.

**Q. What are landfills?**

**A.** *Landfills* are enormous holes where people dump garbage. There are about 6,000 landfills in the United States. We will fill up over half of them in the next 20 years. For example, the Fresh Kills landfill in New York City will have to close by the year 2000 because its mounds of garbage will be 500 feet high—about the height of the United Nations Building!

**Q. How do we make landfills?**

**A.** We usually set up landfills in natural pits where low-lying land is surrounded by hills. Sometimes earth-moving machines deepen the hole and build up the sides. We line the inside of the pit to keep any waste from seeping out. Trucks dump the garbage into the landfill, and tractors spread it around and cover each layer of garbage with dirt.

**Q. How much garbage ends up in landfills?**

**A.** About 80 percent of the garbage produced goes to landfills. We incinerate, or burn, another ten percent. We recycle only ten percent of our garbage. Every American sends an average of four pounds of garbage to a landfill every day.

## Q. What is organic waste?

**A.** *Organic waste* is trash made of things that were once alive. Organic waste can be apple cores, bread crusts, grass clippings, or twigs. Much of the garbage you and your family throw out every year is organic trash.

## Q. What happens when things decompose?

**A.** When garbage or other materials decompose, they break down into simpler parts and rot, or decay. This is nature's way of recycling. Some things, such as food, decompose quickly. Other things, including plastics, can take hundreds of years to decompose.

## Q. How fast does waste decompose?

**A.** Pick four or five pieces of garbage, such as food scraps, a newspaper, a sheet of aluminum foil, some weeds, or a plastic bag. Ask your mom or dad where you might dig a small hole to bury each of these items. Uncover them after a month or so to see which things have begun to decompose. Check again every few months. This will show you how long it takes trash to decompose.

**Q. Why does garbage smell?**

**A.** The bad smell is from the decay of food scraps. The smells come from microscopic organisms, including molds, yeasts, and bacteria. As food scraps break down into simpler substances, they release gases. One such gas is hydrogen sulfide, the bad-smelling gas produced by rotten eggs. Methane is another gas that comes from decaying garbage. Methane has no smell, but it can cause an explosion.

**Q. Can garbage explode?**

**A.** Yes, garbage can explode. But don't worry, this will not happen to your household trash. In landfills, however, vast amounts of rotting garbage are piled in one place. When large amounts of methane gas get trapped underground in the landfill, an explosion can occur. To prevent this, we pipe methane from landfills into furnaces and burn it.

**Q. Can methane gas be used in helpful ways?**

**A.** Methane gas is an energy source. We can burn methane and use the heat to run a steam generator that makes electricity. We can also use methane gas to heat our homes or cook our food.

97

**Q. What happens to chemical products in landfills?**

**A.** Products such as oil, paints, and some cleaners contain harmful chemicals and acids. These products also end up in our landfills. When it rains, water drips through the landfill and mixes with these toxic chemicals.

**Q. What happens to this contaminated water?**

**A.** If the landfill does not have a protective lining at the bottom, the contaminated water could easily leak into the environment. Most older landfills do not have protective linings. Many of them have closed because they are a health threat.

**Q. What happens to garbage when landfills are full or closed?**

**A.** Sometimes garbage has to be hauled in tractor trailers to landfills hundreds of miles away. When a dump in Pennsylvania closed because it was unsafe, the garbage traveled over 600 miles to landfills in Kentucky and Michigan.

**Q. How can you cut down on garbage?**

**A.** Think about the things you do every day that create garbage, and try to find ways to make less of it. Also, remember to reuse and recycle whatever you can. A good way to recycle your family's organic garbage is to make a compost pile.

**Q. What is composting?**

**A.** *Composting* is a process in which you turn organic material that you would normally throw away into a rich mixture that improves the soil and feeds plants.

**Q. What happens in a compost pile?**

**A.** Tiny organisms break down the organic wastes into basic nutrients that then go into the soil. This makes the soil better for plants. If every American family who gardens started a compost pile, about 20 percent of our solid waste would be helping plants grow instead of taking up space in landfills.

**Q. What are decomposers?**

**A.** Worms, insects, mushrooms, bacteria, and other organisms that feed on decaying plant and animal matter are good composters, or *decomposers*. As these decomposers feed on organic waste, they also release many of the valuable nutrients in it and return them to the soil. They break organic matter down into a form that plants can use. Bacteria and fungi are the most important decomposers.

**Q. What do you need to make your own compost?**

**A.** You can buy a ready-made compost container or you can make one of your own. Have your mom or dad help you make a container from wood and wire mesh. Your compost container should be at least four feet long, four feet wide, and three feet tall. Build your container in a sunny spot close to a water supply.

**Q. What goes in your compost?**

**A.** Fill your container with dry outdoor materials, such as weeds, leaves, and grass clippings. You will also need scraps of food, such as banana peels, bread crumbs, coffee grounds, the vegetables you didn't eat at dinner, and egg shells. Avoid cheese, meat, grease, and bones since they can attract pests. Do not add plastic, glass, rubber, or metal.

**Q. How do you make compost?**

**A.** Spread the bottom of your compost pile with coarse material such as twigs, corn stalks, or wood chips. Then add a layer of finer material such as grass clippings or small pieces of kitchen waste. Make each layer about six to eight inches thick. Spread a thin layer of dirt over the garbage and moisten it. Repeat the layers, to a maximum height of five feet. Keep a plastic sheet over the top to hold in heat. Make small cuts in the plastic sheet to let air in. Turn or mix your compost once a week. After a few months, when it is dark and crumbly and has an earthy smell, it will be ready to use.

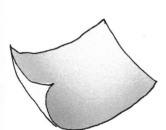

## Q. Where does paper come from?

**A.** Most paper is made from wood pulp, which comes from trees. We use different processes to turn the wood pulp into different kinds of paper, such as newsprint, writing and drawing paper, tissue, and napkins.

## Q. How much paper do people use each year?

**A.** Every year, Americans use 170 billion pounds of paper. Written out, that would be 170,000,000,000 pounds! On average, each person in the United States uses about 580 pounds of paper each year, which is about the weight of a Siberian tiger. Unfortunately, we recycle less than 30 percent of this paper.

## Q. What kinds of paper can we recycle?

**A.** We can recycle many kinds of paper. Some examples are newspaper, notebook paper, copier paper, typing paper, computer paper, index cards, white envelopes, and corrugated cardboard. Be sure to separate magazines from newspapers and to peel any plastic windows from envelopes before you recycle them. Papers with adhesives or coatings are usually not recyclable. Also, you probably won't be able to recycle facial tissues or paper towels.

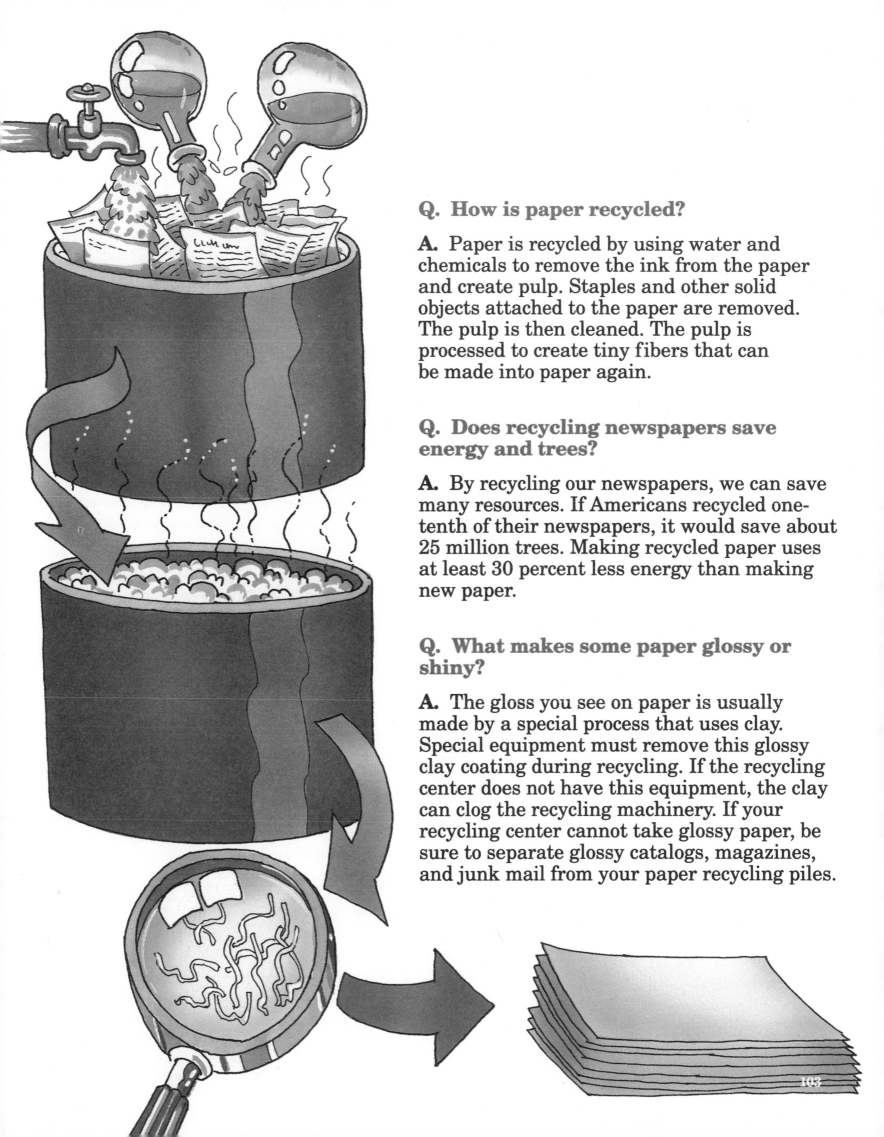

## Q. How is paper recycled?

**A.** Paper is recycled by using water and chemicals to remove the ink from the paper and create pulp. Staples and other solid objects attached to the paper are removed. The pulp is then cleaned. The pulp is processed to create tiny fibers that can be made into paper again.

## Q. Does recycling newspapers save energy and trees?

**A.** By recycling our newspapers, we can save many resources. If Americans recycled one-tenth of their newspapers, it would save about 25 million trees. Making recycled paper uses at least 30 percent less energy than making new paper.

## Q. What makes some paper glossy or shiny?

**A.** The gloss you see on paper is usually made by a special process that uses clay. Special equipment must remove this glossy clay coating during recycling. If the recycling center does not have this equipment, the clay can clog the recycling machinery. If your recycling center cannot take glossy paper, be sure to separate glossy catalogs, magazines, and junk mail from your paper recycling piles.

**Q. What is junk mail?**

**A.** *Junk mail* is unwanted advertising fliers, coupons, requests for contributions, or catalogs that you get in your mailbox. Companies usually send junk mail in the hopes of selling you something. In the United States, junk mail uses about two million tons of paper each year. It often contains glossy paper that is not recyclable.

**Q. Can you do anything to stop getting junk mail?**

**A.** Many times mail order companies sell their lists of names and addresses to other companies. When your family orders from a catalog, you can ask the company not to give your name and address to anyone else. If you receive unwanted junk mail, write the company and ask them not to send you any more.

**Q. How can you help save paper?**

**A.** Recycle your newspapers. Write on both sides of your notebook paper. Reuse paper lunch bags or carry your meal to school in a fabric bag or lunch box. Buy greeting cards that have been printed on recycled paper. Use cloth napkins instead of paper ones and reusable dishes rather than paper plates. Save and reuse cardboard gift and shopping boxes.

**Q. What is the purpose of food packaging?**

**A.** We package food to keep it fresh longer, to protect it from damage or contamination, and to make it convenient to handle, store, and use. The packaging also encourages you to purchase the product by featuring appealing colors, drawings, or pictures. Packaging can provide information, such as the identity of the product, its ingredients, and important nutritional information.

**Q. Was packaging different a century ago?**

**A.** A hundred years ago, products used much less packaging than they do today. Items such as sugar, flour, and pickles came in huge barrels rather than in individual packages. Other items such as candy were kept in large jars and sold one or two at a time. Some items sat on shelves behind a counter and had no packaging at all.

**Q. What materials do we use in packaging today?**

**A.** Today, products come packaged in many ways. Cookies often come in a plastic tray with a plastic wrapper. Juice is sold in cartons, bottles, or small boxes that contain layers of packaging materials and a drinking straw wrapped in plastic. Meats come in plastic foam trays wrapped in a plastic film.

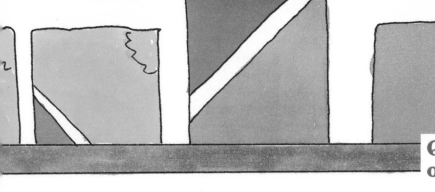

**Q. What problems occur because of overpackaging?**

**A.** When companies try to make their packages bigger and brighter on the supermarket shelves, they often use more materials. This creates waste and costs money. One out of every ten dollars spent on groceries in the supermarket pays for packaging.

**Q. How are some businesses changing their packaging?**

**A.** Some fabric softeners and cleaning liquids come in refill sizes so you can reuse the original packaging. Other products come in concentrated form, which means that you add water to them when you use them. These products come in smaller boxes or bottles.

**Q. How much packaging does your family use?**

**A.** You probably aren't aware of just how much packaging you and your family use in a week. For one week, collect the packaging material you might otherwise throw away in a box or bag. Ask other family members to help you. Find creative ways to reuse and recycle some of the packaging.

**Q. What can you do about overpackaging?**

**A.** Be a packaging detective by noticing the way items are packaged and choosing ones that come in simple, recyclable packages. Whenever possible, have your mom or dad buy bulk sizes of items rather than smaller sizes, which use more packaging. Write letters to companies asking them to reduce their packaging. Recycle packaging whenever you can.

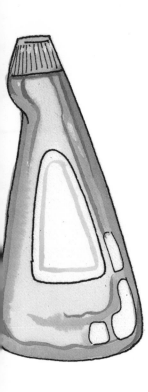

## Q. What is plastic?

**A.** *Plastic* is the name given to any of a large group of substances made from water, limestone, and such materials as coal or oil. People, not nature, make plastics. Nylon and vinyl are plastic.

## Q. What is plastic like?

**A.** Plastic can be clear or colored, hard or soft. It can be molded into many different shapes using pressure and heat. Because it has so many uses, plastic often takes the place of paper, glass, and metal.

## Q. What are some advantages of plastic?

**A.** Plastic does not weigh much so it is easy to carry and transport. It is very sturdy, and it lasts a long time. Plastic makes a strong barrier to preserve and protect things.

## Q. What are some disadvantages of plastic?

**A.** Plastic is made from nonrenewable resources such as oil and coal. Plastic is difficult to recycle. It is not biodegradable, which means it does not break down to become a helpful part of the environment. Much of the plastic we throw away today will be around for hundreds of years.

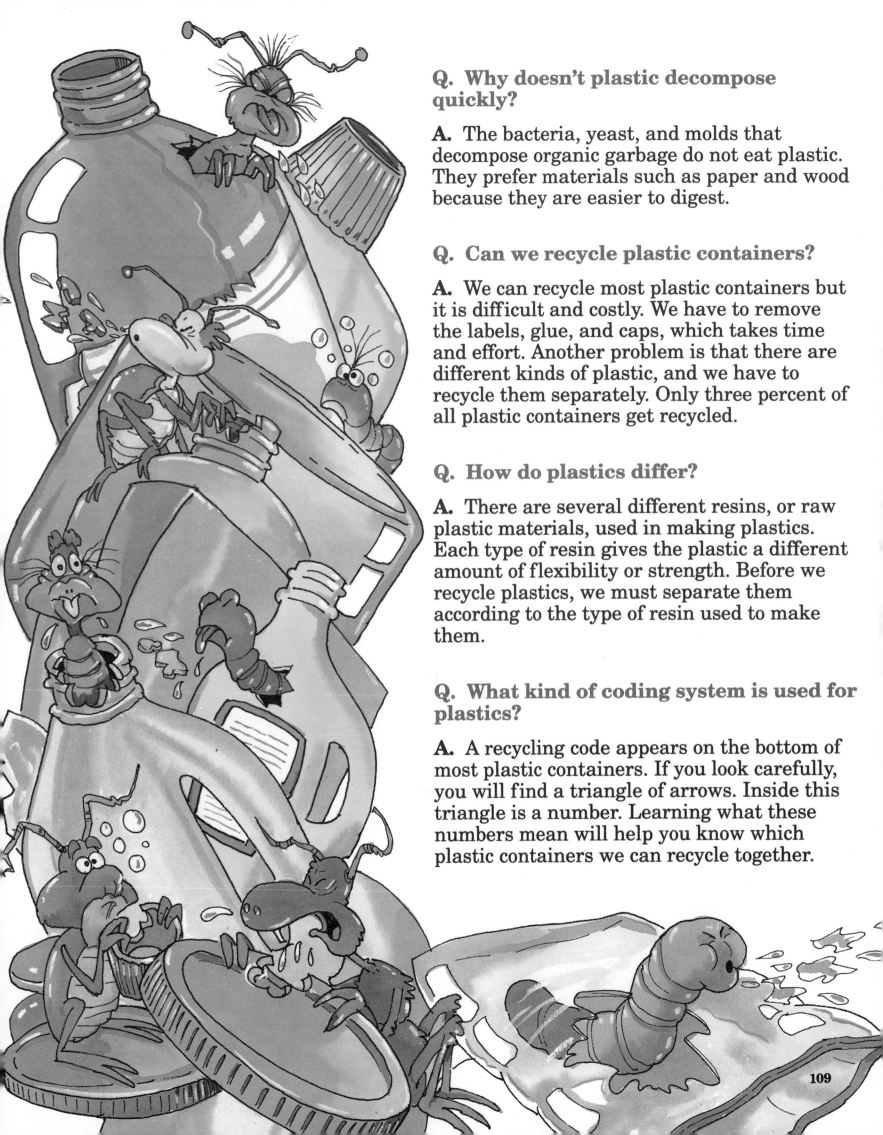

**Q. Why doesn't plastic decompose quickly?**

**A.** The bacteria, yeast, and molds that decompose organic garbage do not eat plastic. They prefer materials such as paper and wood because they are easier to digest.

**Q. Can we recycle plastic containers?**

**A.** We can recycle most plastic containers but it is difficult and costly. We have to remove the labels, glue, and caps, which takes time and effort. Another problem is that there are different kinds of plastic, and we have to recycle them separately. Only three percent of all plastic containers get recycled.

**Q. How do plastics differ?**

**A.** There are several different resins, or raw plastic materials, used in making plastics. Each type of resin gives the plastic a different amount of flexibility or strength. Before we recycle plastics, we must separate them according to the type of resin used to make them.

**Q. What kind of coding system is used for plastics?**

**A.** A recycling code appears on the bottom of most plastic containers. If you look carefully, you will find a triangle of arrows. Inside this triangle is a number. Learning what these numbers mean will help you know which plastic containers we can recycle together.

109

**Q. What does code #1 plastic mean?**

**A.** Code #1 plastic is PET, or PETE. These letters stand for polyethylene terephthalate. This plastic is usually green or clear. We use it as containers for carbonated drinks, peanut butter, and mouthwash. PET containers are easier to recycle than most other plastics.

**Q. What does code #2 plastic mean?**

**A.** HDPE is code #2 plastic. HDPE stands for high-density polyethylene. About 60 percent of all plastic bottles are HDPE, including those containing shampoo, detergent, and juice. Milk jugs and the plastic bags that crinkle loudly are also made from HDPE. HDPE plastic is also easy to recycle.

**Q. What does code #3 plastic mean?**

**A.** PVC is code #3 plastic. PVC stands for polyvinyl chloride. PVC products include floor tiles, credit cards, shower curtains, pipes, garden hoses, and cooking oil containers. Only certain areas accept PVC for recycling.

**Q. What does code #4 plastic mean?**

**A.** LDPE, or low-density polyethylene, is code #4 plastic. We use LDPE for sandwich bags, dry-cleaning bags, shrink wrap, and squeezable containers for foods like mustard and ketchup. Not all areas accept LDPE for recycling.

**Q. What does code #5 plastic mean?**

**A.** Code #5 plastic is polypropylene, or PP. This light plastic is used to make the linings in disposable diapers. It is also in bottle caps, syrup containers, and drinking straws. Polypropylene is usually not recyclable.

**Q. What does code #6 plastic mean?**

**A.** PS, or polystyrene, is code #6 plastic. PS is also known as plastic foam. We make hot-beverage cups and foam pellets used to pack breakable things from PS. We also make containers that hold ointments such as first aid creams from PS. Polystyrene does not decompose; it stays in landfills forever. Also, we use harmful chemicals to make polystyrene. If we burn PS to get rid of it, these chemicals end up in the air.

**Q. Is it better to use paper or plastic bags?**

**A.** Neither is ideal. Paper bags use up trees and plastic bags use up oil. Both kinds often end up in landfills. Talk to your mom and dad about using cloth bags when they go shopping, or at least reusing the bags they get at the store. You can do your part by bringing your lunch to school in a fabric lunch bag or a lunch box.

**Q. What are some ways we can use recycled plastic?**

**A.** Once it is recycled, plastic can be reused in many ways. Recycled plastic is used to make toys, carpet backing, park benches, waste baskets, and fiber filling for ski jackets and sleeping bags.

**Q. How can you help reduce the amount of plastics used?**

**A.** Use products that have no plastic whenever you can. For your next birthday party, do not use disposable plates or eating utensils. Do not use polystyrene products and avoid going to restaurants that do. If you must use plastics, reuse or recycle them.

## Q. What is glass?

**A.** *Glass* is a smooth, hard, clear substance that breaks easily. We use it to make windows, lenses, mirrors, drinking glasses, light bulbs, and bottles. Glass is made from sand, soda ash, limestone, and feldspar. We have to heat these materials and melt them to make glass.

## Q. Why do we use glass for containers?

**A.** We use glass to hold things such as foods, drinks, and cosmetics. Glass doesn't leak, so it makes a good container for liquids. We can also make glass containers in interesting shapes and colors.

## Q. Why is it important to recycle glass?

**A.** Glass containers make up eight percent of the solid waste in American landfills. Every bottle you recycle means one less bottle in a landfill. Some of the materials in glass come from underground mines; digging for them destroys land and uses energy. Recycling glass saves several kinds of natural resources.

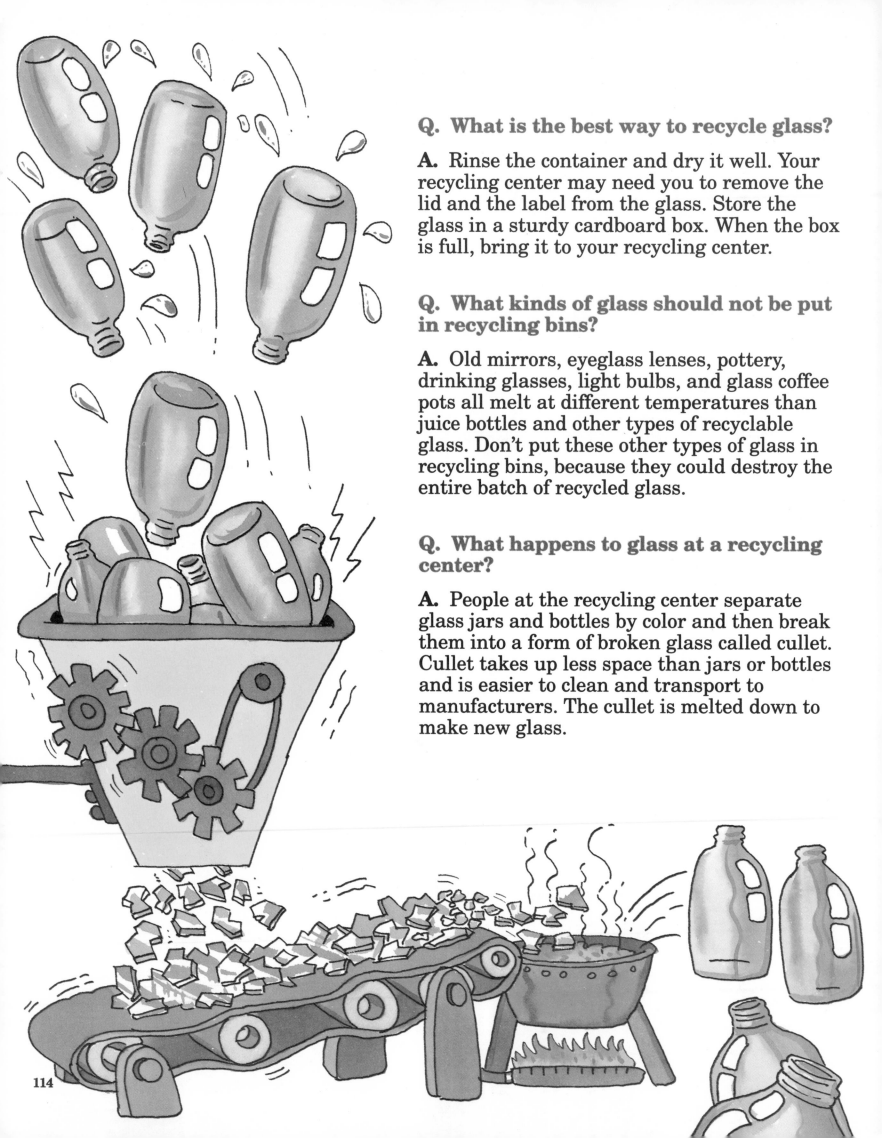

**Q. What is the best way to recycle glass?**

**A.** Rinse the container and dry it well. Your recycling center may need you to remove the lid and the label from the glass. Store the glass in a sturdy cardboard box. When the box is full, bring it to your recycling center.

**Q. What kinds of glass should not be put in recycling bins?**

**A.** Old mirrors, eyeglass lenses, pottery, drinking glasses, light bulbs, and glass coffee pots all melt at different temperatures than juice bottles and other types of recyclable glass. Don't put these other types of glass in recycling bins, because they could destroy the entire batch of recycled glass.

**Q. What happens to glass at a recycling center?**

**A.** People at the recycling center separate glass jars and bottles by color and then break them into a form of broken glass called cullet. Cullet takes up less space than jars or bottles and is easier to clean and transport to manufacturers. The cullet is melted down to make new glass.

**Q. What are refundable glass containers?**

**A.** These containers can be sterilized and reused by manufacturers. They are made of heavy, thick glass. Manufacturers can wash and refill them as many as 30 times. Many beverages are sold in refundable glass bottles. You pay a deposit on each container when you buy it at the store. If you return them to the store, you get your deposit back.

**Q. What are nonrefundable glass containers?**

**A.** Nonrefundable glass containers are made of thinner glass than refundable ones. They weigh less and are easier to carry. Manufacturers can't clean and reuse them, but we can recycle them.

**Q. What are ways you can reuse glass bottles and jars?**

**A.** Put your imagination to work, and you can come up with many uses. Use empty baby food jars at your desk or study area at home to store rubber bands and paper clips. Use empty jars in your family's workshop or garage to hold nuts, bolts, and screws. Use them in the kitchen for spices or in the sewing room to store buttons and spools of thread.

## Q. What is aluminum?

**A.** *Aluminum* is a lightweight, silver-colored metal. It is not very strong by itself. When we use it, we usually mix copper or zinc with it to make it stronger. Aluminum is soft and can take on many shapes.

## Q. What do we use aluminum for?

**A.** Many items in your home contain aluminum. Some examples include soda cans, bicycles, foil, some frozen food trays, and pie plates. Every year, Americans use over 65 billion aluminum soda cans. Every one of them can be recycled.

## Q. How can you prepare aluminum for recycling?

**A.** First, wash out the aluminum cans to keep ants and other insects away. Crush the cans and store them in a box until it is time to recycle them. Be sure to wear shoes if you stomp on them. Always be careful when you handle crushed cans. Sometimes they have sharp edges on them.

## Q. How do we recycle aluminum cans?

A. After aluminum cans are collected, they go to factories where they are ground into small chips. These chips are melted down and made into solid bars. Next, the bars are rolled into flat sheets of aluminum. These sheets go to companies that make cans. New cans are then made from your recycled ones. There is no limit to how many times aluminum can be reused.

## Q. Can you recycle other aluminum products?

A. Aluminum foil, trays, and pie plates are recyclable, too. This kind of aluminum doesn't contain the same material as aluminum cans, so you must separate it from cans for recycling. You may not be able to use curbside recycling for any aluminum other than cans, but many recycling centers will accept all kinds of aluminum.

## Q. How does recycling aluminum help our Earth?

A. When you recycle aluminum, you help to save energy. It takes as much energy to make one new aluminum can as it does to make 20 recycled ones. Also, making one recycled aluminum can will create 95 percent less air pollution than making a new can from raw materials. In 1988, we recycled 55 percent of all the aluminum cans made.

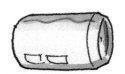

**Q. How can you tell if a can is aluminum?**

**A.** Some cans are made from steel and some are made from aluminum. To tell the difference, hold a magnet to the can. The magnet will stick to a steel can. If the magnet does not stick, the can is made of aluminum.

**Q. Can you recycle steel or tin cans?**

**A.** Tin cans are actually made mostly of steel. They contain a small amount of tin to keep them from rusting. We use these cans for such things as peas, pineapple slices, and dog food. They can be melted down and reused. By recycling steel cans, you save about 74 percent of the energy needed to make them from new materials.

**Q. How is the tin removed from steel cans for recycling?**

**A.** Before steel cans can be recycled, the tin coating must be removed from them. At a special plant, the cans are put in a chemical solution, and an electric current removes the layer of tin. The remaining steel is then ready to be melted down and made into new cans.

118

**Q. How can you recycle toys you have outgrown?**

**A.** Go through your room and find toys and games that you no longer play with. Instead of throwing them away and making more garbage, find a new home for them. Pass the toys and games on to a friend, donate them to a hospital or a school, or sell them at a garage sale.

**Q. Does your school have a recycling program?**

**A.** If it does, keep up the good work. You should feel proud that you and your classmates are doing something good for the environment. If your school doesn't have a recycling program, talk to your teacher or principal about forming a group to start one. Contact your school's PTA for help and support.

**Q. Do your parents have a recycling program at work?**

**A.** If your parents work outside the home, ask if their company has a recycling program. Share with them all that you have learned about recycling. Suggest ways they can recycle at work by collecting office paper, computer paper, aluminum cans from vending machines, and glass.

## Q. What is a pesticide?

**A.** A *pesticide* is a poison used to kill pests such as rodents, insects, or weeds. Farmers and home gardeners want to kill weeds because weeds make it hard for young plants to grow. Rodents and insects can destroy crops and damage plants. Farmers spray about 70 percent of their crops with pesticides.

## Q. What is pesticide residue?

**A.** When farmers use a pesticide, some of the poison stays on the plants. This leftover poison is called *pesticide residue*. Sometimes this residue is still on the fruits and vegetables we buy in the store. Also, when pesticide residue stays on the grains and grass that farm animals eat, it can contaminate the milk, eggs, and meat that come from these animals.

## Q. Where does most pesticide residue in our diet come from?

**A.** The pesticide residue we eat comes from many sources. About 55 percent comes from meat, 23 percent comes from dairy products, six percent comes from vegetables, four percent comes from fruits, and one percent comes from grains.

**Q. How can you avoid pesticides in you diet?**

**A.** For foods such as fruits and vegetables, it is a good idea to rinse them in cold water to remove any traces of pesticides. Whenever possible, eat organically farmed foods, which contain no pesticide residue.

**Q. What is organic farming?**

**A.** *Organic farming* is farming without harmful pesticides or synthetic fertilizers. Organic farms use natural methods to control pests, and they use recycled organic wastes for fertilizer. Organic farms produce food that is better for us to eat, and they do not harm the environment.

**Q. Where can you find organic food?**

**A.** Supermarkets sometimes sell organic foods. If your store doesn't carry any, look for health food stores in your community. Local farmers' markets are another place to find organic foods. Better yet, grow some of your own organic fruits and vegetables in a garden.

121

# AIR & ENERGY

**Q. What is air?**

**A.** *Air* is a mixture of gases. It is made mostly of nitrogen and oxygen, but it also includes small amounts of many other gases. Air is all around you. It is on a mountaintop and in an underground parking lot. Air is in your house, your school, and your car. Air has no color, taste, or smell.

**Q. What is the atmosphere?**

**A.** The *atmosphere* is the layer of air surrounding the Earth. Gravity holds the atmosphere in place. The atmosphere is 310 miles thick, and it has four different layers.

**Q. What are the four layers of the atmosphere?**

**A.** Scientists have divided the atmosphere into four different layers based on temperature. The first layer is the troposphere, followed by the stratosphere, the mesosphere, and the thermosphere. The air in each of the layers is different, but each layer is an important part of the Earth's environment.

**Q. Which layer is closest to the Earth?**

**A.** The *troposphere* is the layer closest to the Earth. It is about ten miles thick. Most clouds, storms, wind, and other weather occur in this layer. The temperature changes more often and more quickly in this layer than in any other.

**Q. In which layer do planes fly?**

**A.** Pilots like to fly in the *stratosphere* so they can stay above snow, thunderstorms, and heavy winds. The stratosphere is about 20 miles thick.

**Q. What is the mesosphere?**

**A.** The *mesosphere* is above the stratosphere. It has the lowest temperatures in the atmosphere. Trails left by meteors appear in the upper levels of the mesosphere.

**Q. What is the thermosphere?**

**A.** The *thermosphere* begins about 50 miles above the Earth and continues until it fades into space. More than 99 percent of our air is below the thermosphere. The air is very thin in this layer of the atmosphere. Because the air is so thin, the sun heats it to very high temperatures.

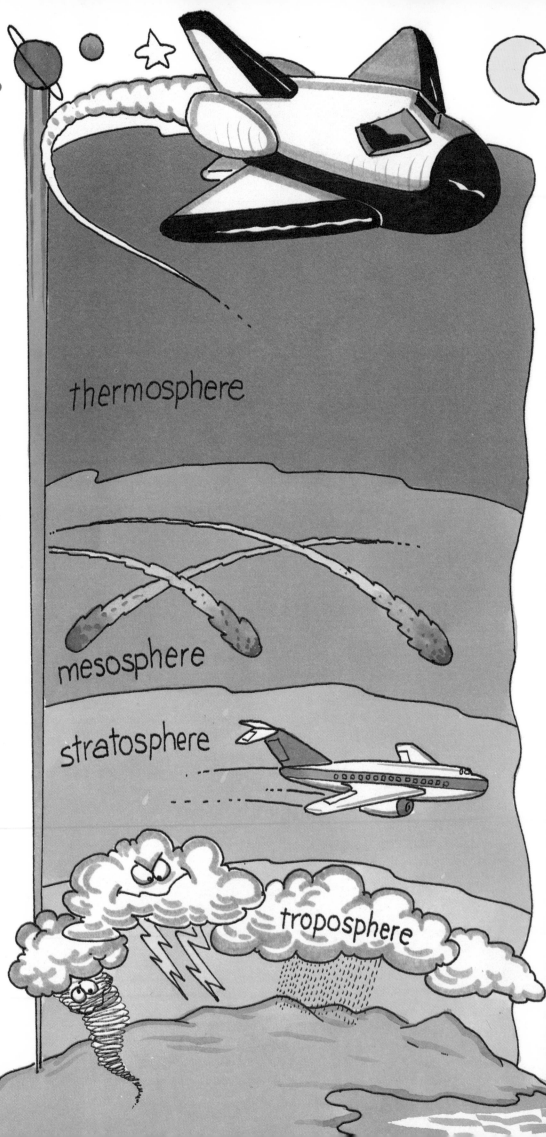

**Q. Why is air important?**

**A.** People breathe air to stay alive. You could survive only a few minutes without air. Air supports the life of all plants and animals living on Earth. The air in our atmosphere also protects our planet from the sun's harmful rays and intense heat.

**Q. What other things can air do?**

**A.** Air carries sound waves. Without air, we would not be able to hear music playing, dogs barking, or people talking. Air is also used to move things. Air can move sailboats across a lake and turn the blades of windmills in grassy fields. You use air to fly a kite, blow bubbles, and inflate a ball. Without even thinking about it, you use air in many ways every single day.

**Q. If we cannot see the air, how do we know it is there?**

**A.** Although you cannot see the air itself, you can see it move other things. Try this simple project. Make a mobile by reusing a wire coat hanger. Cut out six shapes of different lengths from paper scraps. Put a small hole at the top of each one. Attach the shapes to the hanger with some thread or wire. Hang the mobile outside and watch how it moves when air currents hit it.

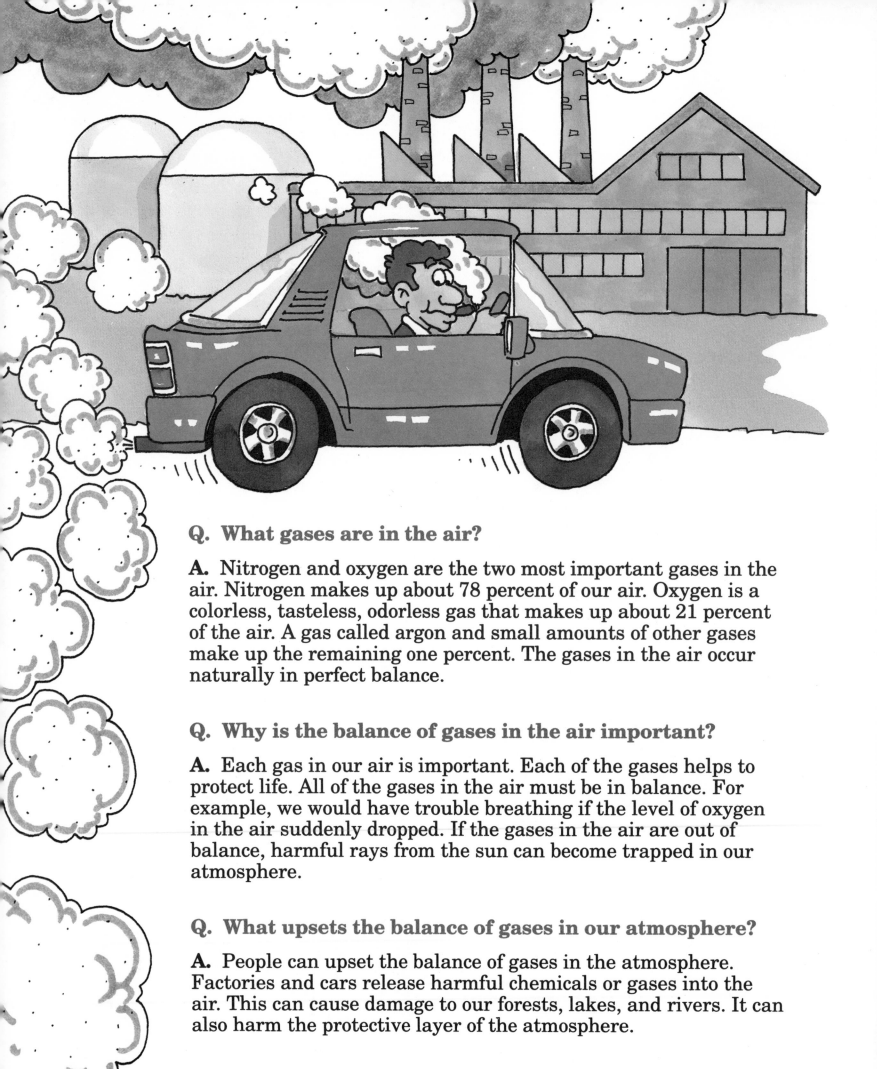

**Q. What gases are in the air?**

**A.** Nitrogen and oxygen are the two most important gases in the air. Nitrogen makes up about 78 percent of our air. Oxygen is a colorless, tasteless, odorless gas that makes up about 21 percent of the air. A gas called argon and small amounts of other gases make up the remaining one percent. The gases in the air occur naturally in perfect balance.

**Q. Why is the balance of gases in the air important?**

**A.** Each gas in our air is important. Each of the gases helps to protect life. All of the gases in the air must be in balance. For example, we would have trouble breathing if the level of oxygen in the air suddenly dropped. If the gases in the air are out of balance, harmful rays from the sun can become trapped in our atmosphere.

**Q. What upsets the balance of gases in our atmosphere?**

**A.** People can upset the balance of gases in the atmosphere. Factories and cars release harmful chemicals or gases into the air. This can cause damage to our forests, lakes, and rivers. It can also harm the protective layer of the atmosphere.

**Q. What was our air like hundreds of years ago?**

**A.** Hundreds of years ago, our air was clean. People woke up each morning to skies that were clear and blue. They walked, or they used horses and wagons to get where they needed to go. They made the things they needed by hand. Children breathed fresh, healthy air. There were no factories, no airplanes, and no cars.

**Q. What happened to our air?**

**A.** With the invention of machines, people began to build factories that sent harmful gases and thick black smoke into the atmosphere. Then automobiles were invented. Cars poured even more pollution into the air.

**Q. What is air pollution?**

**A.** *Air pollution* is harmful waste gases that people release into the air. We can see some air pollution, such as smoke or dust. But there are other harmful pollutants in the air that we cannot see. Air pollution upsets the balance of gases that protects our planet.

## Q. What are the sources of air pollution?

**A.** Cars and buses send exhaust fumes into the air. Smoke from burning leaves, refineries, and factories enters the air in big, gray clouds. Even gasoline-powered lawn mowers cause air pollution.

## Q. Is air pollution a health problem?

**A.** Pollutants in the air can make you sick. When you breathe polluted air, the impurities often stay in your lungs. They can also make your eyes feel watery, itchy, and irritated. They can give you a headache and make your throat feel sore.

## Q. What are other effects of air pollution?

**A.** Pollutants in the air also poison our water and harm fish and wildlife. Air pollution causes $100 million a year in damage to our crops and kills plants that grow near our highways.

## Q. How can you "capture" pollution?

**A.** Attach several pieces of double-sided tape to scraps of cardboard. Place them in different areas around your house: in the garage, in the kitchen, or outside by a tree. After three or five days, check to see if you have "captured" any pollution—dirt and other dark particles on the tape.

**Q. What is ozone?**

**A.** *Ozone* is a special form of oxygen that occurs naturally in a layer in the upper atmosphere. This layer of ozone is important and helpful to our Earth. Some of the pollutants that people produce also form ozone near the ground. When ozone builds up near the ground, it can be harmful to plants and animals.

**Q. What is the ozone layer?**

**A.** The *ozone layer* is about 20 miles above the surface of our Earth in the stratosphere. The layer of ozone in our atmosphere keeps some of the sun's rays from reaching the Earth.

**Q. Why is the ozone layer important?**

**A.** The sun is one of the things that makes life on Earth possible. It's warmth and energy affect our land, our water, our weather, and all living things. The sun also produces rays that are harmful to life, however. The ozone layer is extremely important because it acts as a screen to protect plants and animals from the sun's harmful rays. When the ozone layer becomes thin, we have less protection.

OZONE

**Q. What are the harmful rays from the sun?**

**A.** The harmful rays from the sun are called *ultraviolet rays*. We cannot see ultraviolet rays. In small amounts, these rays are safe and necessary. Ultraviolet rays help your body to make vitamin D. Ultraviolet rays are also what cause you to get a sunburn.

**Q. How are ultraviolet rays dangerous?**

**A.** Large doses of ultraviolet rays can cause severe sunburns, skin diseases, and eye problems. Ultraviolet rays can reduce our ability to fight diseases. In large amounts, ultraviolet rays can damage crops in our fields and tiny plants in our seas that fish need for survival.

**Q. What can you do to protect yourself against ultraviolet rays?**

**A.** If you are going to be in the sun, spread a sunscreen lotion on your skin. These lotions have different numbers on them that indicate the amount of protection they will give you from ultraviolet rays. Talk to your parents about which sunscreen would be best for your skin.

**Q. What are CFCs?**

**A.** CFCs, or *chlorofluorocarbons,* are gases that people have made. They do not occur naturally in the air. CFCs are chemical air pollutants. When these gases reach the ozone layer high in our atmosphere, they can destroy it.

**Q. Why are CFCs bad for the atmosphere?**

**A.** When CFCs reach the atmosphere, they break down the oxygen that makes up the ozone layer. This takes away some of the protection the ozone layer provides. More ultraviolet rays are able to reach the Earth through holes in the ozone layer.

**Q. What do we use CFCs for?**

**A.** For many years, we used CFCs in aerosol cans to pump liquids out in a fine, thin spray or mist. They did not affect the liquid in the can in any way. Many countries, including the United States, no longer use CFCs in most aerosol cans. Other countries have promised to stop using CFCs in aerosol cans soon. There are other sources of CFCs. The CFCs from these other sources continue to harm the ozone layer.

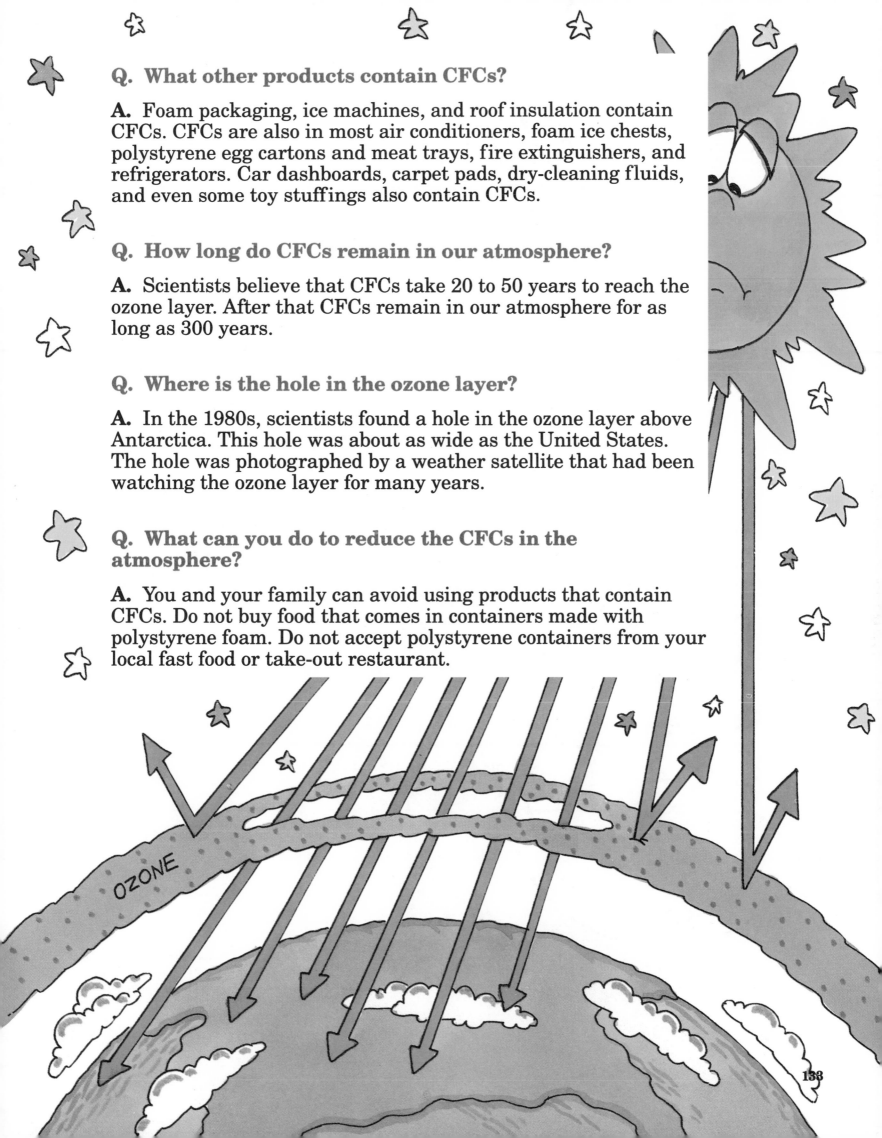

**Q. What other products contain CFCs?**

**A.** Foam packaging, ice machines, and roof insulation contain CFCs. CFCs are also in most air conditioners, foam ice chests, polystyrene egg cartons and meat trays, fire extinguishers, and refrigerators. Car dashboards, carpet pads, dry-cleaning fluids, and even some toy stuffings also contain CFCs.

**Q. How long do CFCs remain in our atmosphere?**

**A.** Scientists believe that CFCs take 20 to 50 years to reach the ozone layer. After that CFCs remain in our atmosphere for as long as 300 years.

**Q. Where is the hole in the ozone layer?**

**A.** In the 1980s, scientists found a hole in the ozone layer above Antarctica. This hole was about as wide as the United States. The hole was photographed by a weather satellite that had been watching the ozone layer for many years.

**Q. What can you do to reduce the CFCs in the atmosphere?**

**A.** You and your family can avoid using products that contain CFCs. Do not buy food that comes in containers made with polystyrene foam. Do not accept polystyrene containers from your local fast food or take-out restaurant.

OZONE

133

## Q. What are fossil fuels?

A. *Fossil fuels* come from a natural process that occurs deep within the Earth over millions of years. This process changes the remains of plants and animals into oil, coal, and natural gas. We burn these fossil fuels to release energy to run our cars, buses, trucks, and airplanes. We also use fossil fuels for making chemicals, generating electricity, and other things. By burning fossil fuels we create exhaust.

## Q. What is exhaust?

A. When cars burn gasoline, they produce *exhaust* gases. These gases contain harmful pollutants. They also contribute to the buildup of a gas called carbon dioxide in the atmosphere. There are about 550 million vehicles in the world, enough to stretch around the Earth about 40 times. The exhaust from all these vehicles pollutes the air and produces harmful ozone near the ground.

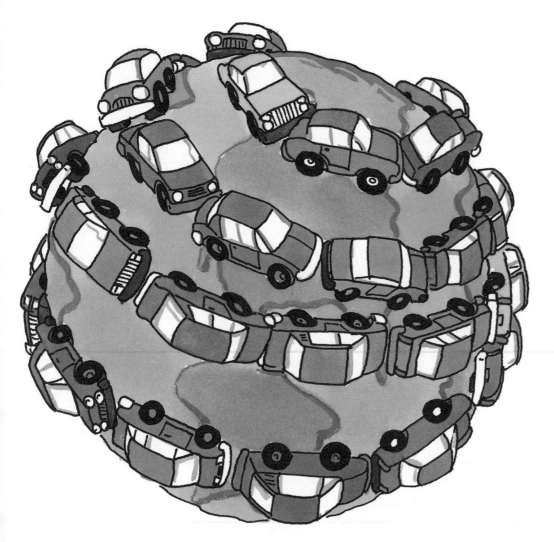

## Q. How can ozone be harmful?

A. Ozone in our outer atmosphere is good, but ozone at ground level is not. Ozone in the air you breathe can irritate your lungs and cause other health problems. It can also damage plants.

## Q. What is smog?

**A.** *Smog* is a combination of smoke and fog. It is a mixture of different pollutants that become trapped near the ground in naturally occurring fog. Smog forms in large cities that have problems with traffic and automobile exhaust. Sometimes you can actually see and smell smog in the air. In large amounts, it can make you sick.

## Q. What happens when there is a lot of smog in the air?

**A.** Smog can cause breathing problems and make your eyes feel sore and itchy. Scientists study the levels of smog in the air. If the smog level is too high, they may issue a "health alert." A health alert advises people who are very young, very old, or sick to stay indoors.

## Q. What is carbon monoxide?

**A.** *Carbon monoxide* is a tasteless, odorless, and colorless gas. It is poisonous to plants and animals. For humans, carbon monoxide keeps blood from carrying oxygen from the lungs to other parts of the body. Automobile exhaust contains carbon monoxide. It is also in home kerosene heaters and cigarette smoke.

**Q. How can you reduce pollution from fossil fuels?**

**A.** A healthy and pollution-free solution is for you to walk or ride your bike instead of riding in a car. Use public transportation if your trip is too far to walk. Join car pools and ride with friends to help cut down on pollution.

**Q. What else is being done about air pollution caused by cars and trucks?**

**A.** Since the mid-1970s, cars driven in America have been designed to use lead-free gasoline. Lead is very dangerous when it is released into the air through car exhaust. Also, all cars must have a device called a catalytic converter. A catalytic converter changes about 90 percent of the harmful gases in car exhausts into less harmful substances.

**Q. How can cars of the future help cut down on air pollution?**

**A.** Car makers are developing cars that run on sources of energy that won't pollute our air. There are even cars being invented that can run on energy from the sun. By making cars that do not burn fossil fuels such as oil and gas, we can help keep our air clean.

**Q. What is noise pollution?**

**A.** *Noise pollution* is filling the air with loud sounds that do not occur naturally. Imagine what you might hear out in the country—birds singing, leaves rustling, insects buzzing, and other sounds of nature. Then imagine what you might hear on a city street corner—horns honking, planes flying overhead, motorcycles revving up their engines. These sounds are a form of pollution.

**Q. What noise pollution is in your home?**

**A.** Stereos blasting, televisions blaring, alarm clocks buzzing, and telephones ringing can be annoying and disturbing. This form of indoor air pollution can have an effect on how you think and feel.

**Q. Is the noise level too high in your home?**

**A.** Sit quietly in your home. Close your eyes for about two minutes. Listen to all the sounds you hear. Notice where they are coming from, and then decide what the greatest source of noise is in your home. Try this test several times. Then think of ways you can reduce the noise levels in your home.

**Q. How clean is the air inside our homes?**

**A.** Surprisingly, some indoor air can have even higher levels of air pollution than outside air. Pollution levels can be as much as ten times higher indoors than they are outside! This does not mean that all indoor air is unhealthy. Even if the air you breathe has some pollution in it, it is usually not enough to bother you or make you sick. But indoor air pollution is a problem for many people.

**Q. What makes indoor air unhealthy?**

**A.** Not all buildings are well ventilated. This means that the air cannot move around well. In some newer office buildings, the windows don't open to let fresh air in. Also, cleaning products and plastics can give off harmful fumes. If large amounts of these things collect in the air, they can make you sick.

**Q. What can you do about indoor air pollution?**

**A.** Ask your parents to stop using oven cleaners, polishes, and kitchen cleansers that produce toxic fumes. Whenever possible, use environmentally safe cleaning products instead of more toxic cleaners. Baking soda, lemon juice, white vinegar, and borax are all safe products that do not add to air pollution in your home.

**Q. Is indoor tobacco smoke dangerous?**

**A.** People burn about 467,000 tons of tobacco each year. Smoke from cigarettes, cigars, and pipes is harmful to the smoker and to anyone else around. Smoke inhaled by nonsmokers is called passive smoke or secondary smoke. This smoke is one of the largest sources of indoor air pollution.

**Q. What is being done to protect people from passive smoke?**

**A.** Many restaurants now set aside special sections for nonsmokers so they do not have to breathe passive smoke. Some businesses are not allowing employees to smoke at their desks or work stations. Airlines make certain flights nonsmoking. Smoking is not allowed in theaters, elevators, and many other enclosed public places.

**Q. What can you do about passive smoke?**

**A.** If anyone in your home smokes, encourage them to quit smoking. Talk to your parents about making a no-smoking policy in your home. Have your parents ask visitors who smoke to please do so outside instead of inside your home. If people do smoke inside your home, ventilate your house by opening as many windows as possible.

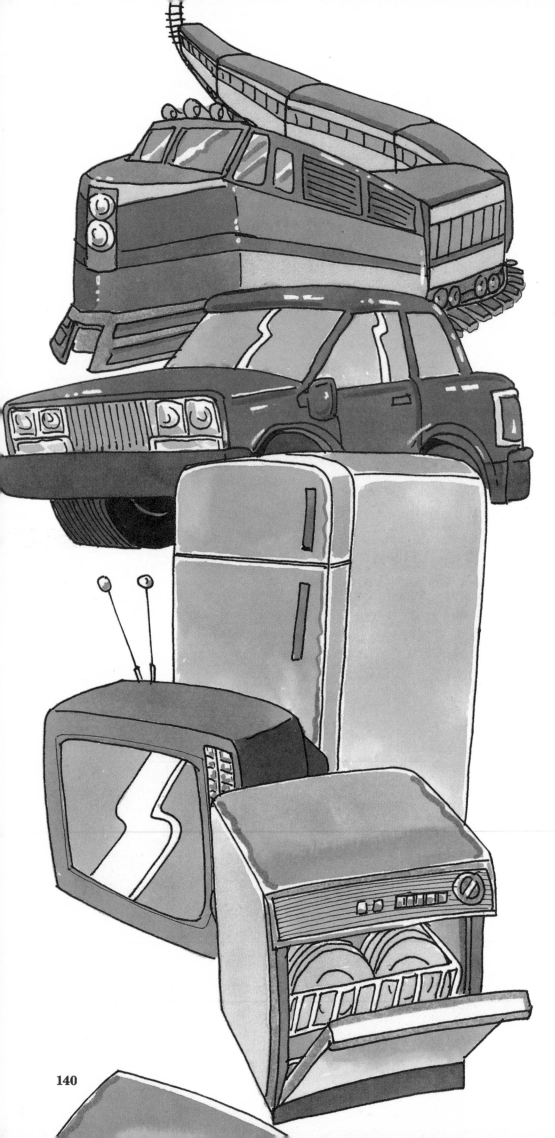

## Q. What is energy?

**A.** *Energy* is the capacity to do work or the ability to make things move. People and animals produce energy from the food they eat. They use that energy to run, walk, think, grow, make noise, and survive. People have also learned how to control energy from other sources.

## Q. What do people use energy for?

**A.** Energy is an important part of our everyday lives. Electric energy in our homes powers our televisions, lights, refrigerators, and other devices. Outside the home, energy powers cars, trucks, and machinery. The United States uses more energy per person than any other nation in the world.

## Q. What are the different forms of energy?

**A.** Many different kinds of energy are available to us. The sun, water, wind, wood, coal, and oil can all make energy. Each kind of energy has its own advantages and disadvantages, or its own good points and bad points.

## Q. What is solar energy?

**A.** *Solar energy* is energy produced by the sun. Devices called power cells can change energy from sunlight into electrical energy. We can also use solar energy to make heat. Solar energy can operate fans, calculators, flashlights, and other appliances in your home. It can also heat water, swimming pools, or even a whole house.

## Q. What are some of the advantages of solar energy?

**A.** Solar energy doesn't pollute our air. It does not harm our environment. Solar energy does not destroy our protective ozone layer. We do not use fossil fuels such as coal, gas, or oil to make solar energy.

## Q. What is a disadvantage of solar energy?

**A.** The amount of solar energy we can use depends on the amount of sunlight that is available. On a cloudy day, we have less solar energy than we do on clear days. At night, we have no solar energy. Scientists are looking for ways to store solar energy so we can depend on it all the time.

**Q. What is wind energy?**

**A.** *Wind energy* relies on the force created by blowing winds to generate power. Wind is a renewable resource, unlike coal, oil, and other fossil fuels. Wind energy does not pollute our air.

**Q. What is a windmill?**

**A.** A windmill is a machine that works using power from wind. A windmill is made of blades attached to a central pole. When strong winds hit the blades, they turn and cause the pole to turn, too. The wind energy captured this way can generate electricity.

**Q. Where were windmills first used?**

**A.** Windmills were first used long ago in what is now Iran for grinding grain. Later, Europeans used windmills to power pumps that drained water from the land. Americans used windmills in the early 1900s to generate electricity.

**Q. What are wind farms?**

**A.** Wind farms are rows of windmills built on acres of flat or gently rolling land. The energy captured when wind turns the blades of the windmills generates electricity. People are studying new ways to use windmills and capture wind energy.

142

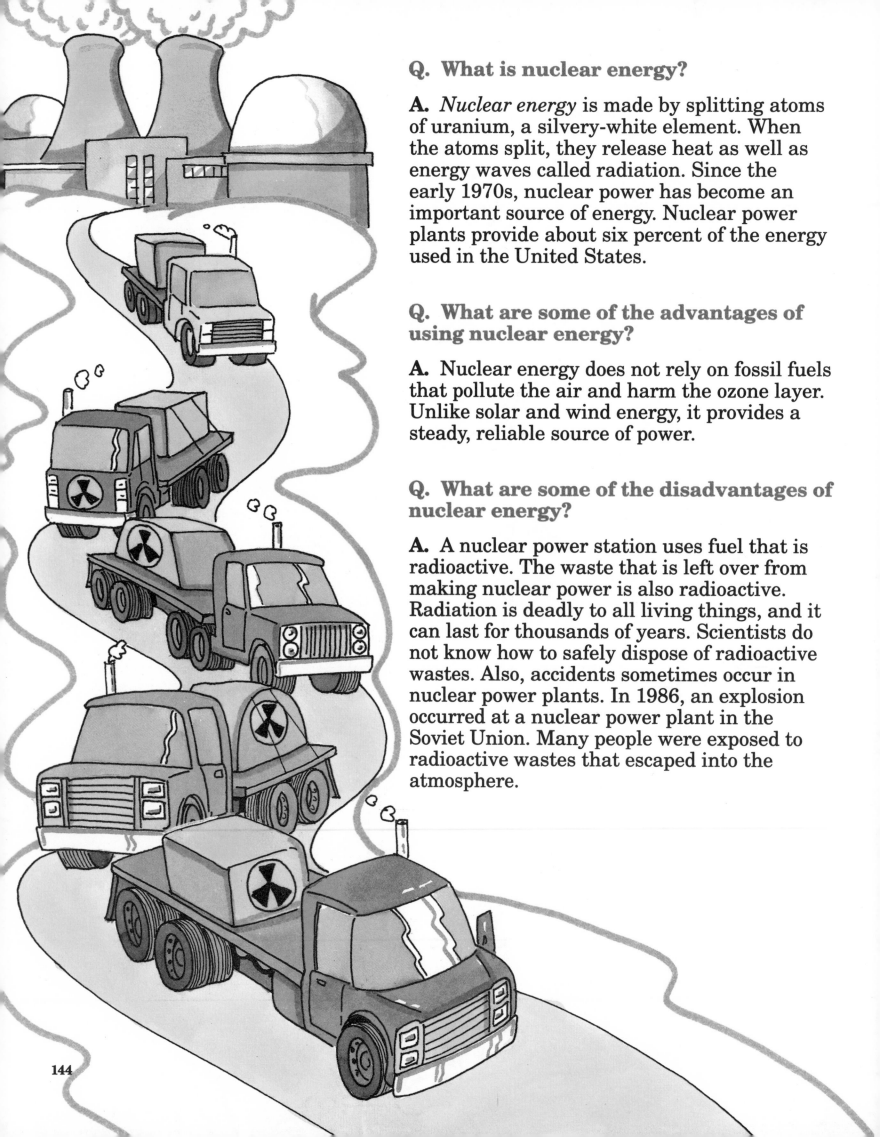

**Q. What is nuclear energy?**

**A.** *Nuclear energy* is made by splitting atoms of uranium, a silvery-white element. When the atoms split, they release heat as well as energy waves called radiation. Since the early 1970s, nuclear power has become an important source of energy. Nuclear power plants provide about six percent of the energy used in the United States.

**Q. What are some of the advantages of using nuclear energy?**

**A.** Nuclear energy does not rely on fossil fuels that pollute the air and harm the ozone layer. Unlike solar and wind energy, it provides a steady, reliable source of power.

**Q. What are some of the disadvantages of nuclear energy?**

**A.** A nuclear power station uses fuel that is radioactive. The waste that is left over from making nuclear power is also radioactive. Radiation is deadly to all living things, and it can last for thousands of years. Scientists do not know how to safely dispose of radioactive wastes. Also, accidents sometimes occur in nuclear power plants. In 1986, an explosion occurred at a nuclear power plant in the Soviet Union. Many people were exposed to radioactive wastes that escaped into the atmosphere.

**Q. What is petroleum?**

**A.** *Petroleum* or oil is a liquid found underground in the rocks that form our Earth's crust. It is a fossil fuel because it comes from the remains of plants and animals that have decomposed. Petroleum ranges in color from clear to black. It is a nonrenewable resource.

**Q. How do we use petroleum today?**

**A.** Petroleum is very useful. Over 3,000 things we use every day come from petroleum. Some of these include records, tires, paints, ink, eyeglasses, plastic, dishwashing liquid, and deodorant. Petroleum is even used in bubble gum!

**Q. How is petroleum harmful to the environment?**

**A.** Sometimes when people move oil, they spill it. Oil pipelines can leak. Sometimes oil trucks are involved in accidents, and they spill oil over freeways and highways. Ships carrying oil can tear their hulls on rocks and pour oil into the sea. When we spill oil into our seas and on our land, it causes serious damage to the environment.

## Q. What is a greenhouse?

**A.** A *greenhouse* is a glass building used to grow plants. The glass walls of a greenhouse let sunlight in and then trap its heat inside and make the greenhouse warm. A greenhouse provides a safe and warm home for growing plants, even when the weather outside is cold. In many ways, the atmosphere of our Earth is like a greenhouse.

## Q. What is the greenhouse effect?

**A.** Some gases in the Earth's atmosphere act like a greenhouse. The gases let sunlight through and then trap some of its heat. This natural *greenhouse effect* warms the Earth just enough for plants and animals to live here.

## Q. What are the greenhouse gases?

**A.** *Greenhouse gases* such as methane and carbon dioxide trap heat near the Earth. They are a natural part of our atmosphere. People also make greenhouse gases. When we burn coal and oil, for example, we make tons of carbon dioxide. These extra gases build up in the atmosphere. This traps more heat and makes the Earth warmer.

**Q. What is global warming?**

**A.** *Global warming* is the slow rise in the Earth's temperature. One cause of global warming is the greenhouse effect. If the world's average temperature rises just a little, conditions all over the world could change and cause problems for every living thing. Some areas could turn into desert, and others could become permanently flooded.

**Q. When will we feel the effects of global warming?**

**A.** Global warming will not happen all of a sudden. We will not see its effects in the next few months or years. Even though the most harmful effects may not happen in our lifetime, we should learn about global warming and try to stop it.

**Q. How can you help stop global warming?**

**A.** You can help stop global warming by cutting down on the use of fossil fuels. Walk or ride your bike if you can, instead of riding in a car. When you do this, you use less fuel and create less greenhouse gases. Planting a tree will also help. Trees remove carbon dioxide from the air. This lessens the greenhouse effect and fights global warming.

**Q. What is a battery?**

**A.** A *battery* is a container with materials that make electrical energy by chemical reaction. We use batteries to power toys, clocks, radios, and cars. Batteries can contain lead, mercury, sulfuric acid, and zinc. These chemicals are toxic or poisonous.

**Q. What happens to batteries that wear out?**

**A.** When batteries wear out, people throw them away. Americans throw out about 2.5 billion pounds of batteries a year. These batteries often end up in landfills. The poisonous chemicals inside can leak out and contaminate the soil and the water.

**Q. What are rechargeable batteries?**

**A.** Most of us use disposable batteries. When they can no longer produce energy, we throw them away. When we use up the energy in a *rechargeable battery*, we can plug it into an electrical outlet recharge it, and use it again.

**Q. How can we use batteries in a safe way.**

**A.** Turn off your battery-operated devices when you are not using them. Use rechargeable batteries, or buy things that do not need batteries at all, such as solar-powered calculators. Call your recycling center for information on how to dispose of batteries.

**Q. What is electricity?**

**A.** *Electricity* is an important form of energy. Electricity produces heat and light. Electricity provides power to run your toaster, your dishwasher, and the television in your home. Electricity also provides the power for radios, computers, ovens, refrigerators, telephones, and air conditioners.

**Q. Where do we get our electricity?**

**A.** People produce electricity at power plants using large machines called generators. We burn coal or oil to make steam. The steam provides the energy to run the generators, and the generators make the electricity. Wires then carry this electricity to homes, factories, and businesses.

**Q. How many electrical gadgets do you have?**

**A.** Make a list of all the electrical gadgets that you and your family have for convenience: can openers, pencil sharpeners, toothbrushes, and carving knives. When these things break or wear out, consider replacing them with things you operate by hand. Every bit of electricity you save also saves energy.

149

**Q. What are ways you can save energy in your home?**

**A.** Most American households waste half the energy they use. Get into the habit of checking a room before you leave it. Turn the lights, television, and radio off when you leave a room. Ask your family to make these energy-saving steps a habit.

**Q. What are compact fluorescent light bulbs?**

**A.** *Compact fluorescent bulbs* use less energy to operate than the standard light bulbs most people use at home. Compact fluorescent bulbs cost more to buy, but they last much longer. An average standard light bulb can burn for about 375 hours. A compact fluorescent bulb lasts about 7,500 hours, or 20 times as long.

**Q. How can you use less energy to heat your house?**

**A.** Twelve times more heat escapes through a window than through a wall. Close your curtains at night to help keep the heat inside your room. Talk to your mom or dad about putting weather stripping tape around windows to help seal in the heat and keep cold air out. Your parents can also buy windows that help keep heat inside. Ask your parents to lower the heat in your home. If you feel cool, put on a sweater instead of turning up the heat. If you keep the temperature a bit lower, your furnace uses less energy.

**Q. How can we save energy with our refrigerators?**

**A.** The temperature of your refrigerator should be between 38°F and 42°F. Ask your mom or dad to adjust the setting if it is set below 38°F. Each time you open your refrigerator door, the cold air inside escapes into your warmer kitchen and the refrigerator has to use energy to make it cold again. Try to open the door less often and for less time. Ask your family to keep track of how many times they open the refrigerator door for a day. Talk about ways you can reduce the number of times you open the refrigerator.

**Q. How can we save energy with our ovens?**

**A.** When you peek inside the oven to check on something cooking inside, heat escapes. You waste energy because more power is needed to heat the oven back up again. Resist the urge to open the oven door just to see what is inside.

**Q. How can you save energy when you boil water?**

**A.** Keep a lid on the pot when you are boiling water. The lid traps heat in the pot instead of letting it escape, and the water boils faster. More of the energy from the stove goes toward heating the water, and less gets wasted.

**Q. What are some other energy-saving tips for the kitchen?**

**A.** Remind your mom or dad to bake with glass or ceramic pans whenever possible. They keep in more heat than metal pans. If your family uses an electric stove, the bottom of your pan or pot should be about the same size as the burner it is sitting on. You waste energy by cooking with a small pot placed on a large burner.

**Q. Can you use cold water in your washing machine?**

**A.** Heating the water in a washing machine takes a lot of energy. Up to 90 percent of the energy used for washing clothes goes to heat the water. Ask your mom or dad to wash clothes in warm water and to use cold water for rinsing. This will save energy and clean your clothes.

**Q. Where is the lint screen in your clothes dryer?**

**A.** When the lint screen on your dryer gets clogged, your dryer uses more energy to do its job. Ask your mom or dad to show you where the lint screen is and how to clean it. On your family's next wash day, ask your parents if you can be responsible for cleaning the lint screen. Or better yet, hang your clothes to dry outside and don't use your dryer at all!

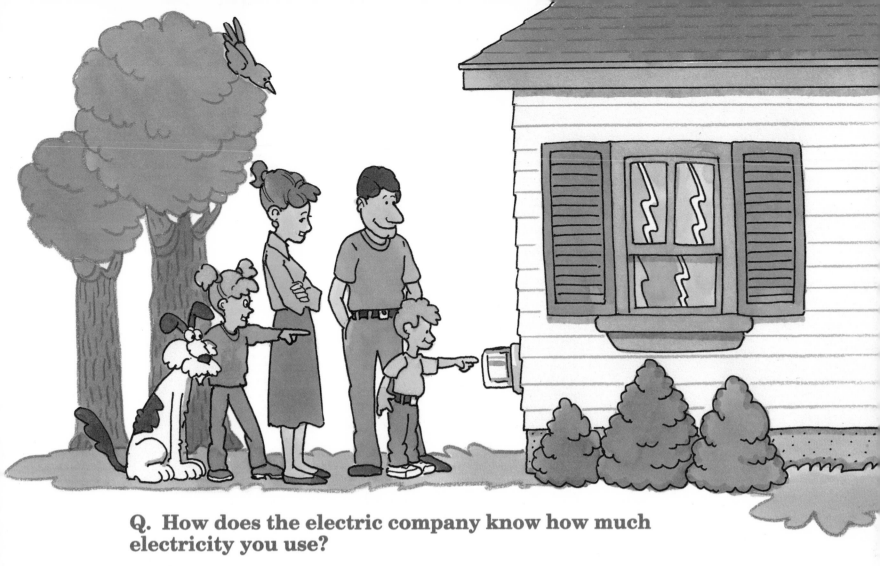

**Q. How does the electric company know how much electricity you use?**

**A.** The line that brings electricity to your home has a meter on it. The meter measures the electrical energy you and your family use. An employee of the power company reads this meter regularly. The electric company bases your bill on what the meter says.

**Q. Where is the meter for your house?**

**A.** Ask your mom or dad to show you where your electric meter is. Notice how many dials there are. The meter reader uses the numbers on these dials to see how much electricity you and your family use.

**Q. How can people use energy more wisely?**

**A.** We can use energy more wisely by using less of it. We can turn out lights, turn down the heat, and use our cars less often. We can also work to find cleaner ways to make energy. By using energy wisely, we can conserve our natural resources and cut down on the pollution we produce. There is a lot to be done. But there is also a lot everyone can do to help.

# TAKING ACTION

**Q. What can you do to make a difference?**

**A.** You can help the environment in many ways. You can learn about the environment and then share what you learn with family members, classmates, and friends. You can write letters to express your opinion or to ask for information. You can take action and get involved in projects that will help our Earth.

**Q. How can you learn more about the environment?**

**A.** Read! Many books and magazines can teach you how plants and animals live and how nature works. As you discover the beauty, wonder, and excitement of nature, you will begin to respect and appreciate our world more. Other books deal with problems—pollution, global warming, hazardous wastes, and endangered animals. They will help you learn how to take care of the Earth. Read the newspaper to learn about environmental problems around the world and in your area.

**Q. How can you let other people know how you feel about the environment?**

**A.** You can write to the editor of your local newspaper, the president of a nearby company, or the manager of your recycling center. You can write to government leaders who can make changes that will help the environment.

**Q. How can you let businesses know you care about the environment?**

**A.** Write to the president of a company that is doing something nice for the environment and say thank you. It is important to let businesses know you appreciate their efforts. You can also write to the president of a company that is not doing its share to help heal the Earth. In your letter, let that person know how you feel. Ask if the company plans to do things differently in the future.

**Q. What can you ask government leaders to do?**

**A.** When you write to an elected official, explain your concerns about the environment. Ask them what they are doing about a specific problem. Ask if there are any laws they could sponsor or support that might help the problem. Let them know you will share any information you receive with your family and friends.

**Q. What government leaders can you write to?**

**A.** You can contact any elected official through the mail. In your own community, you can write to the mayor or members of your town or city council about the environment. You can write to the governor or your state legislators. There are many laws affecting the environment that are passed by states. You can write to members of Congress and even to the President of the United States.

**Q. How can you send for information about the environment?**

**A.** Many organizations work to encourage recycling, to save endangered plants and animals, and to clean up the environment. Look in your local library or in the phone book under "Environmental Organizations" for the names and addresses of these organizations and write to some. Tell them about your interest in their work. Ask them to send you information so you can learn more about what they are doing to help the environment.

**Q. What might these organizations send you in the mail?**

**A.** Many organizations will send you booklets, pictures, and other worthwhile information. Others will send you copies of their newsletters or magazines. They will tell you how you can become involved in their efforts to help the environment.

**Q. What can you do with the information you receive?**

**A.** Read and study the information you get. Share what you learn with your family and friends. Put the material inside a folder so you keep it organized. It might come in handy for a school project or report later on. If you find any of the organizations especially interesting, you may want to join.

157

**Q. How can you help the environment?**

**A.** Talk with your mom and dad about the environment. Discuss how you and your family can help by using water wisely, sorting your trash for recycling, and using the other ideas presented in this book. Participate in community environmental events such as Earth Day.

**Q. Can you make holidays more environmentally safe?**

**A.** On Valentine's Day, make your own valentines out of recycled paper. If you have a picnic on the 4th of July, ask your parents to bring reusable plates and cups. When you go trick-or-treating on Halloween, use a pillowcase for collecting your goodies instead of paper or plastic bags. During Hanukkah and Christmas, reuse wrapping paper instead of buying new paper.

**Q. Can you give gifts that help the environment?**

**A.** For birthdays and other occasions, you can give subscriptions to an environmental magazine. Consider giving gifts that will help the environment such as a bird feeder or a colorful reusable lunch bag. You can also plant a tree or make a donation to an environmental organization in someone's name as a special gift.

**Q. How can you start an environmental club?**

**A.** Ask friends in your neighborhood and classmates at school to join you in starting an environmental club. When people work together and share ideas, they can often do more than one person working alone. An environmental club is also a way of having fun with your friends while you are helping the Earth.

**Q. How do you decide what your club will do?**

**A.** At the first meeting, let the members talk about the environmental problems that are most important to them. Make a list of the problems and pick one issue from the list for your club to focus on. Find a project that will help that problem in some way. You could raise money to help save a rain forest. You could write letters to save a neighborhood park. You could start a recycling program at your school.

**Q. How can your club accomplish its goals?**

**A.** Once your club has a project, you need to develop a plan. Talk about different ways you can meet your goals, and pick out the best ones. Then assign specific jobs to everyone in the club. Talk to parents and teachers to see if they can offer any suggestions or help. You could also go to government officials or local businesses and ask them for help and support.

**Q. What are some environmental careers?**

**A.** Many people who care about the Earth choose jobs that help the environment in some way. Some of these people are biologists, lawyers, forest rangers, geologists, legislators, organic farmers, and recycling engineers. If you are interested in these careers, read about them. Try to meet some people who work in these jobs. In the future, you might make a career of helping the Earth, too!

**Q. How can you make every day Earth Day?**

**A.** We can make every day Earth Day by turning lights off when we leave a room, recycling our trash, working to save endangered animals, writing letters about our concerns to people who make the laws, and having respect for nature in all we do.

**Q. Can you really make a difference?**

**A.** Absolutely! Every time you do something for the Earth, it *does* make a difference. When you snip the plastic six-pack rings from soda cans, you might save the life of a marine animal. When you recycle waste, you save energy and natural resources. When you teach others about the environment, you might get them to join together to protect our Earth.